NATURE GUIDE TO FLORIDA

Nature Guide to Florida

550 subtropical plants, birds, marine and animal species
illustrated in color and described in text

By Richard Rabkin and Jacob Rabkin

Banyan Books
Miami, Florida

Library of Congress Cataloging in Publication Data

Rabkin, Richard, 1932-
    Nature guide to Florida.

    Includes index.
    1. Natural history--Florida. I. Rabkin, Jacob,
joint author. II. Title.
QH105.F6R3   500.9759   78-23491
ISBN 0-916224-44-9

All illustrations by the authors.

Manufactured in the United States of America

CONTENTS

To DOROTHY

from her son and her husband

INTRODUCTION

This book is not a scientific treatise or an identification manual. However, science has not been ignored nor have appearances been distorted. The primary objective of the book is to turn some of the attention of residents and visitors of all ages to the ecological wonders that can be observed with relative ease and enjoyed with minimum effort in this subtropical climate. Therefore, you are given overall impressions of the various environmental units that dominate the landscapes. The drawings, though not always to scale, will help in recognizing the illustrated species. The text is a verbal extension of the drawings, summarizing data from personal observation and reasonable research. The book will serve its purpose if, from time to time, it stimulates you to notice and appreciate the miraculous ways of life in the fields and prairies, forests and swamps, seashores and beaches, marshes, mudflats, streets, and gardens of south Florida.

1. GEOGRAPHY AND GEOLOGY

The area of Florida south of Lake Okeechobee is a vast wonderland of subtropical flora and fauna. It is the borderland between the tropical West Indies and the temperate zone to the north. Much of the landscape is dominated by water: the Atlantic Ocean, the Gulf of Mexico, the Big Cypress Swamp, the Everglades, Florida Bay, Biscayne Bay, and the numerous lakes, rivers, sloughs, and coastal swamps and marshes that are so visibly a part of the landscape. Other parts of the landscape are vast sandy prairies and flatlands covered in many places by extensive pine forests. Bordering the Atlantic Ocean is the so-called coastal ridge—the narrow strip of slightly elevated land on which the major cities of eastern Florida have been built. In the main, however, the entire region is flat, featureless, and low in elevation, with a unique geography and an interesting geological history.

In terms of world geography the northern boundary of the tropics is an imaginary line known as the Tropic of Cancer. This line runs around the globe immediately north of Cuba. No part of the Florida peninsula lies within this tropical zone; all of the state is in the temperate zone. Yet, the climate of Florida, particularly the southern portion, is nearly tropical, that is, subtropical, with wet humid summers and fairly cool, dry winters. This climate occurs because the natural forces that create the weather are oblivious to boundary lines. The most significant of these forces are generated by the Atlantic Ocean and the Gulf of Mexico. These large bodies of water moderate the climate of the peninsula, preventing extremes of heat and cold. In addition, the warming influence of the Gulf Stream and of the prevailing winds from the Caribbean help to produce gentle winter weather. These factors keep Palm Beach, Fort Lauderdale, Key West, and Sarasota all comfortably mild and pleasant, while such places as Cairo, Taipei, Karachi, and Kuwait, which are located on approximately the same parallels, are baked and blasted by a merciless sun.

Geologically, Florida is the youngest part of the nation. What we now see as the land mass of the state is the portion of a large, submerged table that rises above the present sea level. The submerged area, an extension of the continental land mass that is referred to by geologists as the Floridan Plateau, is approximately equal in size to the visible area that forms the state. If the sea level were lowered about 300 feet, this submerged platform would be entirely exposed, extending almost 100 miles west of Sarasota but only a short distance from Miami. This geological feature has played a significant part in the birth and formation of the state.

The principal physical features of Florida were laid down during the so-called Ice Age (the Pleistocene)—the most recent geological period—which began a million or so years ago and has continued right up to the present epoch. A basic fact of geology is that the level of the sea has constantly fluctuated up and down and is still rising and falling. With the beginning of the Ice Age much of the ocean waters of the world became locked in enormous polar glaciers that covered the Arctic and Antarctic zones. When these glaciers formed, the sea level dropped, and large portions of the earth formerly under water became exposed. The entire Floridan Plateau was laid bare. When the ice sheets melted, the sea level rose, and again the plateau became flooded. The great glaciers melted and froze a number of times, with the resulting withdrawal of water during glacial ages and its release during interglacial periods.

During the interglacial periods, the waves of the rising waters left visible evidence of each submergence in the form of distinct marine terraces on the shorelines. Geologists have located eight such terraces, showing that at one time the sea level rose as high as 270 feet above its present level and that during successive interglacial periods the old shorelines were left inland as the sea levels at each stage became lower and lower. About 100,000 years ago, before the beginning of the most recent Ice Age, the sea rose about 25 feet above its present level, high enough to cover almost all of southern Florida. The sea level lowered again during the last (Wisconsin) Ice Age, exposing all the Floridan Plateau. But when these last glaciers melted for the last time and began their retreat, they released enough water to shrink the Floridan Plateau to about half its former size and to bring the sea to its present level and Florida to its present dimensions.

The deep layer of limestone rock that makes up most of Florida's surface is a product of the shallow, calcium-rich sea that covered great sections of the peninsula during the various geologic ages. In the main this rock was formed from the accumulation of the shells and skeletons of dead marine organisms that were deposited on the floor of the sea and that were ultimately compressed into solid rock when the sea receded. In the analysis of the limestone rock of south Florida, geologists have found two distinct types of formation. In the Atlantic coastal ridge the rock is largely composed of billions of tiny spheres. Each of these spheres has a small, sandy nucleus surrounded by layers of calcium carbonate. During the various geologic ages, tier upon tier of these calcareous (i.e., made of calcium carbonate) grains filtered down to the bottom of the sea. When the sea level fell and rainwater percolated down into these exposed inorganic deposits, the chemical reaction bound the loose grains together to form solid limestone rock. Because these calcareous grains have the appearance of fish roe, they are known as "ooids." The rock made of these grains is called "oolite," or oolitic limestone, and it is this porous rock that eventually became the dominant component in the Atlantic coastal ridge.

West of this area, in the low-lying region of the Everglades, the limestone, in addition to the ooids, contains preponderant areas of rock that have had organic origin. This rock started with shells of calcium carbonate secreted as places in which to live by unimaginable billions of minute marine animals known as bryozoans. The remains of these shells produced immense flats that eventually emerged as land and, as in the case of the oolitic mound, gradually became consolidated into hard limestone rock through precipitation caused by rainwater. Although other substances, such as the calcareous tubes of different types of marine worms, also may be components of limestone rock, the major ingredients in south Florida limestone are the oolitic rock of the Atlantic coastal ridge and the bryozoan rock of the Everglades, which together are called Miami limestone.

Geologists generally divide southern Florida into six major physical or natural regions: (1) the sandy flatlands; (2) the Atlantic coastal ridge; (3) the Big Cypress Swamp; (4) the Everglades; (5) the coastal marshes and mangrove swamps, and (6) the Florida Keys. The sandy flatlands are part of the coastal lowlands. The latter are a series of marine terraces extending down both sides of Florida. These terraces meet northwest of Lake Okeechobee and then surround the lake on the east and west, merging on the south on one side with the saw grass Everglades and on the other with the Big Cypress Swamp.

The Atlantic coastal ridge, sometimes called the rim of the Everglades, rises slightly from the Everglades. The majority of the state's population is concentrated in the communities located on this eastern ridge, obviously chosen by the original settlers because of its proximity to the Atlantic Ocean, its elevation, and its relative freedom from periodic flooding and seasonal mosquitos.

The Big Cypress Swamp is a low-lying area of approximately a million and a half acres that spreads out west of the Everglades and grades slowly down into the coastal marshes of southwest Florida. Although much of this vast expanse is covered with swamps that are flooded during the rainy season, slight elevations in the land produce distinct differences in vegetation. In some places where low outcroppings of limestone appear, the landscape is dotted with semitropical tree islands known as hammocks.

The Everglades, which begins below Lake Okeechobee and extends southward into the swamps and salt marshes of the Gulf of Mexico and Florida Bay, is a broad, watery depression 30 to 40 miles wide and more than 100 miles long. The whole expanse is a complex natural phenomenon dominated by thick growths of saw grass, streaked by swales, sloughs, and creeks, and dotted with many small tree islands. The most southwesterly portion of this region, approximately 2,000 square miles, is now the Everglades National Park. Beginning on the east coast at about Cape Canaveral and going around the southern portion and up to Cedar Key on the Gulf of Mexico, there is a fringe behind the sandy beach consisting of saltwater marshes and forests of mangroves and associated plant growth.

The Florida Keys are a chain of small islands rising only about 5 to 10 feet above high tide and extending in a southwesterly arc for about 150 miles from Soldier Key in the north to Key West. Like most of southern Florida, the rock formations of the Keys are limestone. The limestone of the upper Keys, however, is a coral reef rock known as Key Largo limestone, while the lower Keys are made of the Miami limestone found on the mainland.

Because of its geographical location, just south of the temperate

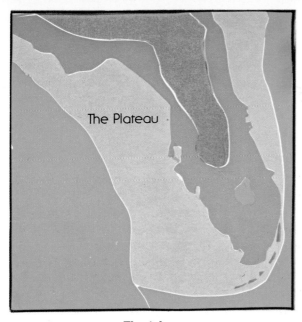

The Plateau

Florida

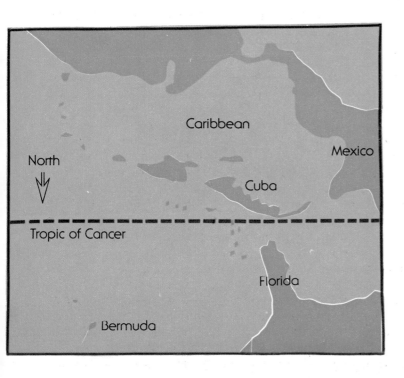

North

Caribbean

Mexico

Cuba

Tropic of Cancer

Florida

Bermuda

Generalized Surface Features of South Florida

Sandy Flatlands

Lake Okeechobee

Prairies

Big Cypress Swamp

The Everglades

Atlantic Coastal Ridge

Mangrove Swamps and Coastal Marshes

Florida Keys

Geography and Geology

land mass and just north of the Caribbean, Florida has become a crossroad where the two different communities—the temperate zone and the tropics—have interacted to produce a remarkable diversity of plant and animal life. Much of Florida has only newly emerged from the sea, providing a wide variety of ecological niches for which the species from both communities constantly compete. The woods, flats, swamps, ridges, hammocks, marshes, and coastal strands teem with this dynamic spectacle.

2. SEA WRACK

The endless drift line of debris left behind by every high tide is the sea wrack. Part of it is man-made and apparently harmless—an old sneaker, a beer bottle or an empty lotion tube. Some of it, like the leakage and discharge from coastline vessels and shoreline refineries—death traps for fishes, birds, and intertidal animals—shows up on the beaches as globs of tar. Most of it, however, is the refuse of plant and animal life in the sea.

Seaweed, the large marine form of algae, makes up the most colorful part of the tide line debris. Seaweeds are classified in part on the basis of color: blue green, green, brown, and red. The blue green seaweeds, made up of microscopic plants, form a dark, slippery scum or a velvety fuzz on rocks, piles, and boat bottoms, and therefore are not part of the sea wrack. Green seaweeds require strong sunlight. They are much more delicate than most of the brown or red varieties. Torn bits of the bright green sea lettuce, *Ulva*, the largest of the green algae, are very common. The frond is a thin, silky, flat membrane with a ruffled margin. Another green seaweed that grows luxuriantly in tropical waters is *Caulerpa*, an important food for turtles. The frond consists of a prostrate stem, from the upper side of which branchlike, secondary fronds arise. Of the many varieties of seaweeds, the most abundant on the east coast beaches is the light brown sargassum, famous because it floats over large areas of the Sargasso Sea. The decomposition and recycling of all the seaweed is carried on by microscopic organisms, e.g., bacteria, fungi, viruses, and others.

Along with the seaweed, which conserves its water by massing together, the tide casts up a great deal of other waste matter. Among all of this the breeding and foraging activities of flies, beetles, bugs, and other insects goes on endlessly. The live and decaying matter in the sea wrack provides food for sand hoppers, crabs, wolf spiders, and others. Clouds of sand hoppers feed on the dead matter, and wolf spiders come out from their tunnels to prey on the insects. Much of this feverish activity occurs at night, when skunks and raccoons come to the water's edge to join the other hunters. During the day, birds invade the windrows (the rows left by the wind or water), probing in the seaweed for mollusks, crustaceans, and worms cast up by the tide.

For many people the most exciting objects on the beach are the seashells. All beachcombers know that the best time for shelling is at low tide, but many look only along the water's edge, ignoring the wealth of specimens in the sea wrack. Although the east coast beaches furnish an ample variety of shells, shelling is often spectacular on the beaches of the west coast of Florida between Sarasota and Everglades City, especially on Sanibel, Captiva, and Marco islands. In these areas a combination of tides and currents dislodges great quantities of mollusks. The lower Florida Keys have a high percentage of colorful West Indian species.

The invertebrate animals that produce seashells all fall into the major group called Mollusca. The word mollusk is derived from the Latin word meaning soft. A mollusk has a soft, unsegmented body that is usually protected by one or two hard, external shells. The shell is secreted by the animal itself, which keeps enlarging it until the animal is fully grown. The shells are called valves. Mollusks with two shells are bivalves; those with one shell are univalves. Mollusks fall naturally into five classes: the chitons, the tusk or toothshells, bivalves, univalves, and the class that includes the squid and octopus. By far the largest class of mollusks are the univalves, with about 80,000 living species. The second largest group, with about 20,000 living species, are the bivalves.

Every shore has its own collection of shells that distinguishes it from other shores, and the sophisticated collector knows precisely where to look for special prizes. Generally, however, many of the more common Florida shells often can be found on shores on both sides of the state. Among the easily spotted shells are: the smooth and highly polished sunrise tellin with wide pink rays; the small, brownish Florida hornshell with speckled white dots in spiral rows; its companion, the long, tapering, yellowish brown common Atlantic auger; the Florida worm shell, sometimes called old maid's curl, found in spongy seaweed masses; the flat-shaped limpet, whose strong muscular foot enables it to adhere to firm objects during the roughest weather; the strong-shelled turkey wing with red brown markings in a zigzag pattern; the thin, fragile, fan-shaped pen shells, which are often covered with slipper shells, the inside of each divided by a small horizontal platform that looks like the quarter-deck of a ship; and the light brown olive shell with an overlay of darker brown. The little clam that creates considerable activity at the tide line is the coquina. It comes in all colors of the rainbow and in a variety of patterns and is normally found in pairs. The calico scallop is a favorite among collectors also because of the great variety of its colors. Among the larger and more spectacular shells are the common fig shells, the tritons, the helmets, the cowries, the whelks, and the conchs.

There are also exotic treasures to be found on the beaches. Among the shells, sponges, coral, driftwood, and seaweed, each tide may bring into the east coast, and occasionally into the gulf side, seeds of various tropical plants. These seeds (disseminules) are carried by the Gulf Stream to the Florida beaches, mainly from the Caribbean region. They are all generally referred to as "sea beans"; although there are almost 100 species, those in greatest demand are the saddle bean, nicker bean, sea bean, and sea heart. At one time the art of carving and polishing sea beans was fairly popular. Today sea beans are primarily other assets in the inventory of the beachcomber.

Among the many other items of great interest on the beaches are the egg cases of various animals of which the so-called Devil's pocket-book, the egg case of the skate, is an example. There are vase sponges, tube sponges, and finger sponges—the latter with their long, reddish brown branches; there are brittle stars, sea urchins, sand dollars, and starfish; there are various species of jellyfishes, including the stinging

Portuguese man-of-war; and there are the skeletons and carapaces of hermit crabs, mole crabs, and calico crabs. Also trapped in this multitude may be the residue of other life in the deeper, pelagic regions, carried to the shore by winds and currents. All of it is nature's "flotsam and jetsam," the floating and jettisoned remnants of the ocean's debris.

Few beaches are without sandpipers, seen in flocks wheeling and twisting in a graceful choreography of their own or running after a retreating wave on twinkling feet and retreating as the next one comes in. The least and semipalmated sandpipers are among the small, streaked species called "peeps." It is difficult to distinguish one peep from another, but the yellow legs of the least sandpiper set it apart from the black legs of the semipalmated. The western sandpiper is generally to be found in the mud flats.

Gulls and terns are everywhere. Their long, narrow, pointed wings make them good fliers, and their webbed feet good swimmers. In summer the laughing gull has a black hood. In winter its head is white. The distinguishing feature of the ring-billed gull is the narrow black ring around its yellow bill. Terns are generally smaller than gulls, with long, pointed wings and forked tails. Most of their food is fish caught by diving headlong into the water. The royal tern is a large bird, distinguished from the smaller ones by its large, orange bill. The least tern is very small, with a yellow bill and black cap. One of the most common terns is Forster's tern, but this bird is more often seen in the salt marshes, not on the seashore.

Next time you visit the shore, discover the treasures to be found in the sea wrack.

3. PELAGIC WORLD

Pelagic sea life consists of the community of plants and animals in and around the surface of deep blue waters. One of the most fascinating pelagic areas is found in the Sargasso Sea, which is not a body of water as the name seems to imply, but rather an immense, floating mass of sargassum seaweed. The enormity of this accumulation was baffling during the days of the sailing ships. Some ancient mariners who came upon this undulating prairie believed it to be a lost land, and legends claimed ships were slowed down and even sucked under by the floating carpet. In fact, these weeds are so dense at times that they impede navigation. On the east coast of Florida a strong northerly wind will drive

thick windrows of the floating weed onto beaches, enriching the inventory in the sea wrack. In these masses of seaweed are enmeshed many of the marine animals that live in or around the blue waters of the sargassum community.

This vast acreage of yellowish brown vegetation is held together by weak ocean currents. The source of this immense mass of seaweed puzzles botanists. The most generally accepted explanation is that the weed lives a pelagic life, that it has dispensed with any root or anchoring device, and that it propagates by division while afloat, with each separated piece forming a new clump. The species of sargassum, abundant in the Gulf Stream between the Bahamas and Florida, can be differentiated from other seaweeds in that it more nearly resembles a

Sea Wrack

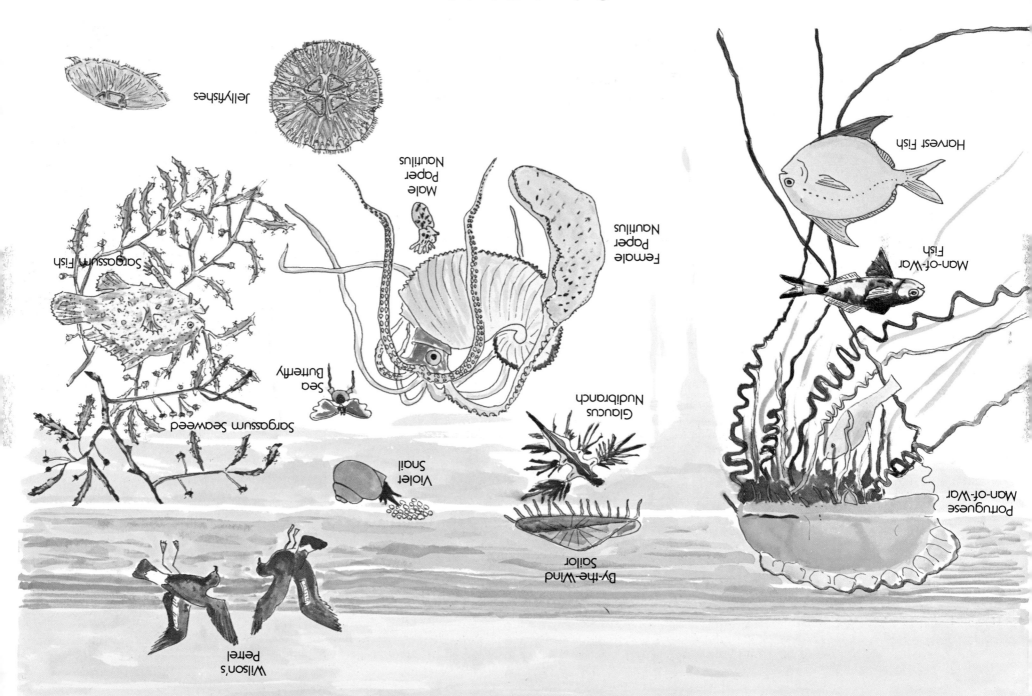

Pelagic World

Jellyfishes

Male Paper Nautilus

Female Paper Nautilus

Harvest Fish

Man-of-War Fish

Sargassum Fish

Sea Butterfly

Sargassum Seaweed

Glaucus Nudibranch

Violet Snail

Portuguese Man-of-War

By-the-Wind Sailor

Wilson's Petrel

true leaf and stem. Its leaf is attenuated and sharply toothed, but its most striking characteristic is the protrusion of small air bladders that give the plant the buoyancy necessary to support itself and its numerous inhabitants.

Countless organisms live and breed in the protective shelter of the floating weeds, such as the minute hydroids (jellyfish), bryozoans (sea lace), barnacles, and anemones. A number of fishes lay their eggs on the floating sargassum. The protective shelter provides a perfect nursery for many small pelagic animals, including the harvest fish. Full-grown dolphins feed mainly on juvenile fishes associated with sargassum, such as flying fishes, filefishes, triggerfishes, and jacks. Some creatures avoid potential predators by adaptations that produce a defensive camouflage. One of nature's very successful camouflage artists is the sargassum fish (*Histrio*), a small fish that grows up to eight inches in length. The mottled coloration matches the environment in which it lives. The golden rings on its sides resemble the distinctive air bladders of the sargassum. It even has developed flexible fins, which look like the branches and leaves of the seaweed and which can be used as arms and fingers to enable it to clamber about its habitat. *Histrio* has a voracious appetite, which it can easily satisfy because it approaches its prey not in the form of a fierce attacker but in the guise of a harmless weed.

Another class of animals that has developed remarkable protective resemblances is the nudibranches. Although they are true mollusks, they do not have shells. Because their bodies have a wormlike appearance they are commonly known as "sea slugs." They are wonderfully beautiful animals, brightly colored and exquisitely shaped. The silvery blue species, called the blue glaucus, has tentacles graduated in size that project from each side. It frequently inhabits clumps of sargassum, crawling and feeding among the fronds. Among its food sources are those jellyfish that have stinging cells, each a poison-filled thread with a sharp point. The blue glaucus has the remarkable ability to convert these stinging cells into its own arsenal of defensive armament. This secondhand armament and its unpleasant taste protect this shell-less slug, which otherwise would be easy pickings for would-be predators.

The blue and delicately pink balloon which is seen floating in tropical and semitropical waters and which frequently is driven onto the beaches in large numbers is the Portuguese man-of-war (*Physalia*). On the upper side of the prominent balloon is a crest, or sail, and from the underside hangs a cluster of streaming tentacles. Some of these tentacles are covered with stinging cells, some tentacles perform feeding functions, and others are the reproductive organs. A fish entangled in this mass is paralyzed by the venom in the cells of the stinging tentacles, which then retract and serve the victim up to the mouths of the feeding tentacles. Although these colonies cannot swim, they are carried along in the water by currents and winds, and the stinging cells retain their potency long after they are washed up on the beach. Despite its threat to both man and fish, *Physalia* is no menace to the so-called man-of-war fish (*Nomeus*), a small blue and silver parasitic fish that navigates with impunity for food and shelter among the mass of tentacles accompanied at times by young harvest fish.

The sea wrack will often contain a small relative of *Physalia*, the by-the-wind sailor (*Velella*). This, too, is a colony of specialized individuals that drifts upon the surface of the ocean, with appendages having different functions of feeding, stinging, and reproducing. It has a bright blue flattened float with a triangular sail extending diagonally across the top. In the seaweed on the beach it dries to resemble a wispy piece of white plastic.

One of the animals that feeds upon *Velella* is the violet snail (*Janthina*), another inhabitant of the open sea. It rides the waves, held up by a cellophanelike float constructed of bubbles of air trapped in a gelatinous substance. As with other pelagic animals, its blue and violet colors provide some camouflaging protection from predators. Because the shell is very fragile, it is difficult to find a perfect specimen in the sea wrack.

Another creature of the open sea, whose empty shell is occasionally washed ashore, is the common paper nautilus or argonaut. The female has two highly modified arms that secrete a parchment-white "shell" into which she deposits her eggs. The male, rarely ever over half an inch in size, has no shell and is less than one-tenth the size of the female. The argonauts swim or drift near the surface of the water in the vast population of tiny sea butterflies, the so-called flying snails, which form a great part of the planktonic animals upon which argonauts and other pelagic creatures depend for their food.

Overlooking the whole empire are the pelagic birds, among which are the small storm petrels, such as Wilson's petrel. They flutter over the waves, pattering their webbed feet on the water, feeding on small fishes, mollusks, crustaceans, and the whole planktonic community. Most of us, however, know the pelagic world only by those bits and pieces of its integrated life that occasionally reach the sea wrack.

4. MIDDLE BEACH

The entire expanse of land from low tide to the top of the sand dune is often called the beach. In fact, however, this area consists of four separate regions. Between the low-tide and the high-tide marks is the intertidal or surf zone, where bursting waves, churning sand, and scouring stones create a violently destructive turbulence. Despite this turbidity, a staggering abundance of microscopic organisms lives near the surface of the water or between the grains of wet sand. The remaining area divides naturally into the middle beach, the dune, and the hammock above the dune.

The middle beach is the battleground of a perpetual struggle between the sea and those plants that grow along the shoreline. The sea is not alone in this battle; it has some formidable allies. The baking sun can produce unbearable temperatures. Showers of salt spray, which can draw water out of the living tissue of plants, add their briny destructiveness. Winds whip up the loose sand that blasts and defoliates some plants and uproots and destroys others. The combination of salt, sand, sun, and storm creates a deadly challenge to most plants, and only those with special characteristics and habits can survive.

Salt spray when caught by the wind can be deposited a considerable distance from the shoreline. Plant adaptations to combat this lethal adversary take forms somewhat similar to those seen in desert species. Some plants have a glossy or waxy surface that prevents the absorption of the salt. Others have stiff leaves that cling tightly to the branches; whatever is accumulated on the leaf surfaces of these plants is washed away by the next rain. In some cases the leaves are protected by a covering of tiny hairs on which the salt spray crystallizes. When the spray stops the hairs dry out and the salt crystals drop to the beach. Some plants fight the loss of water by virtually dispensing with their leaves—those leaves they do possess have been reduced to spines. Other plants store water in fleshy leaves and stems. One species drops its leaves in a severe storm and puts on a new set when calm weather returns. Many of the plants, however, never adjust completely to the hostile elements, and instead of achieving full growth they survive only in a stunted or misshapen form.

Nearest to the water's edge, where the environment is most oppressive, nature starts with very low-growing plants. In this front line the dominant plants are those that can develop into ground covers. The roots and underground shoots of these plants begin the task of binding and stabilizing the sand. The most colorful of these is a vine with three popular names: beach morning glory, goat's foot plant, and railroad vine. It is a trailing plant, with very long, angular, smooth stems and thick, rather succulent leaves. The morning glory name comes from the showy, three-inch, funnel-formed purple flower, the goat's foot from the shape of the leaf, which is two-lobed and notched at the tip, and the railroad part from the heavy vines that run rampant up and down wide stretches of the beach in more or less parallel lines resembling train tracks.

Another common vine, usually several yards long, is the bay bean. Its thick leaflets are in groups of three, and its pea-shaped flower has a rose purple color. Its fruit is an oblong pod that opens when ripe, showing mottled brown beans. Another sprawling plant is the beach peanut, not related to the edible peanut. The stems and branches are fuzzy and sticky so that they attract sand particles, its leaves are in pairs, and its small flowers are deep violet. The urbanization of many coastal areas has driven the beach peanut into the endangered category.

Further up on some beaches are the succulents—the plants that can survive because they have the capacity to store water. Sea purslane is a vinelike, perennial herb with fleshy, spatulate (shaped like a spatula) leaves, and long stems that crawl on the sand. This is one of the most common sea strand plants. Marsh elder is a low, shrubby plant, woody at the base but producing rather succulent, broad leaves. Another plant with a woody base is the many-branched spurge, whose fleshy stems discharge a milky sap.

Behind the first line of plants are those that have the appearance of straw. The tallest is sea oats, a stout, profuse, perennial grass that grows as high as seven feet out of dense clumps. It has strong underground stems that anchor and bind the sand in place. Its large clusters of flat seed pods wave majestically in the breezes at the tip of elongated blades. These clusters are strikingly ornamental, but sea oats are protected and may not be removed in Florida primarily because its subsurface stem system helps to bind the sand. Another deeply based plant is the tall beach grass, whose underground stems perform the same stabilizing function as sea oats.

Beach star, a small herb with a close cluster of overlapping, grass-like leaves, also has elongated, creeping underground stems. Crowfoot grass, sometimes called Egyptian grass, is a soft-stemmed grass generally with five bristlelike spikelets that spread out radially.

Still further up on the beach, near the base of the dune, is the beach sunflower, an excellent ground cover and sand binder whose branches sprawl loosely over the ground. Its irregularly toothed leaves are nearly triangular in shape. Its flower is very showy—a dark brown center surrounded by bright yellow petals. The beach sunflower will often

Spanish Bayonet

Beach Sunflower

Beach Star

Beach Grass

Crowfoot Grass

Sea Oats

Railroad Vine

Ghost Crab

Sea Purslane

Okenia (Beach Peanut)

Bay Bean

Marsh Elder

Spurge

Sand Hopper

Middle Beach

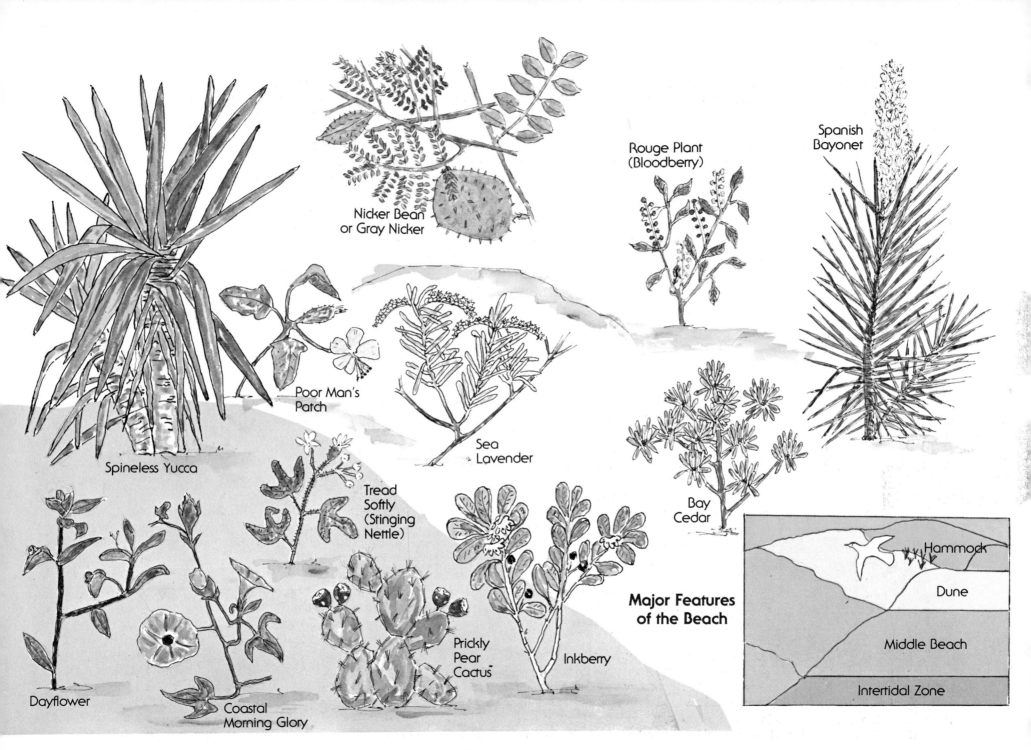

Spineless Yucca

Nicker Bean or Gray Nicker

Poor Man's Patch

Sea Lavender

Rouge Plant (Bloodberry)

Spanish Bayonet

Bay Cedar

Dayflower

Coastal Morning Glory

Tread Softly (Stinging Nettle)

Prickly Pear Cactus

Inkberry

Major Features of the Beach

Hammock

Dune

Middle Beach

Intertidal Zone

Dunes

extend its coverage up along the sand dune, and in its general vicinity the attractive white- or rose-colored flowers of the periwinkle are constantly in bloom.

The struggle is difficult enough when these plants have to contend solely with natural forces. It becomes particularly difficult, though, when man-made jetties, sea walls, and waterfront condominiums are introduced into the conflict. What is left then of many of the so-called beaches becomes a barren wasteland where only scant vegetation can survive.

Life on the beach is equally inhospitable for the animal kingdom. Few can survive in the baked open expanse, composed of quartz particles mingled with shell and coral fragments. Many animals have adapted to this hostile homeland by burrowing underground. These include ants, wasps, spiders, and sand hoppers. One of the more interesting is *Ocypode*, the ghost crab or sand crab. Its common names are derived from its ability to blend so well with the surrounding sand that it becomes difficult to see. Its vulnerable eyes recede into protective cavities at the first threat of danger. Its leg span is almost ten inches, and when frightened it can scurry across the sand with remarkable speed and then disappear into its burrow. The entrance to its burrow is often marked by a pyramid-shaped mound. The ghost crab can manage in this environment because it has a water supply at the bottom of its burrow, and because it has the capacity to store water inside its shell to avoid drying out. It also has ready access to the teeming food supply in the sea wrack, where it competes with other feeders.

The most abundant of the burrowing animals is the shrimplike sand hopper, also known as the beach flea. Some sand hoppers live higher up on the beach, hiding in burrows during the hot day and coming out only at night in search of food.

5. DUNES

Without the sand-hugging plants of the open beach area there would be no dunes. Nature needs three components for the construction of a dune: wind, sand, and an obstruction. The function of the obstruction is to slow the wind and cause some of the sand grains carried by the wind to be dropped. A piece of driftwood or a rock will often suffice. Generally, though, a dune begins with a tuft of leaves that sprouts from one of the horizontal stems of those plants that creep along the beach. A small mound is anchored by the plant. The long, creeping, underground runners of another plant add their binding strength. The mound now provides a greater obstacle to the wind. Larger quantities of sand are deposited and the mound begins to go higher as new shoots of the ground-hugging plants extend themselves to bind another layer of sand into position. In time, and under the right conditions, this over-lapping process produces a dune—a valuable storm-protecting barrier for inland inhabitants.

Living conditions for plants and animals become much more toler-able on the dune. High, storm-driven waves are no longer a threat. The destructiveness of wind-blown sand and salt is blunted. The increased density of the vegetation provides a protection of its own, making the rigorous adaptations for living on the beach no longer necessary. Nevertheless, the threat of desiccation from wind and sun is endless, especially for plants in the front line of the dune. One of these plants is the sprawling cactus known as prickly pear. This plant copes with the problem of prolonged drought by reducing its leaves to spines, thus exposing a minimum of evaporating surface to the sun, and by storing water in its fleshy, connecting segments. It produces a bright yellow flower and an edible, dark red, pear-shaped fruit.

A fine example of a plant that protects itself against dehydration is Spanish bayonet. Its glossy, wax-covered leaves retain water. The stem of these plants, from 8 to 20 feet high, is densely covered with stiff, bayonet leaves that taper to a needlelike point. It bears many glistening, white, fleshy flowers that are edible when fresh, and it produces a bitter but edible purple fruit. The fiber of its leaves is used for cordage. The spineless yucca, a member of the same family as Spanish bayonet, is native to Central America, but is now widely planted in Florida. It produces similar flowers and fruit. Its leaves are smooth and straplike without terminal spines, and its thick stem can attain a height of 30 feet.

A number of different shrubs inhabit the upper reaches of the beach and the dunes. Sea lavender or sea sage, a native to south Florida, grows in huge mounds. The narrow, fleshy, compact leaves are covered with tiny white hairs that give the plant a silvery gray appearance, which is in sharp contrast with the surrounding green vegetation. These hairs protect the leaves against the salt spray. Small white flowers in dense, one-sided spikes grow out of the terminal rosettes. Bay cedar, another native plant, is also a bushy shrub. It has paddle-shaped, fleshy leaves that are covered with fine hairs and that form clusters at the ends of the twigs.

Another shrub that often builds up extensive colonies is inkberry. It has thick, succulent, spatula-shaped leaves and is easily known by its flowers. These white, wavy-edged flowers have five lobes all on one side, spreading out like a fan and giving the appearance of a half-eaten flower.

The shrub known as nicker bean or gray nicker is very evident on the upper part of the dune because it grows like a huge vine, forming great tangles often reaching into tall branches of nearby trees. Its leaves and stems are liberally set with hooked spines. Its upright clusters of yellow flowers are followed by seed pods. These pods are also covered with spines and enclose hard, glossy, bluish-gray seeds. The plant with the prominent raceme of numerous red berries is bloodberry or rouge plant.

Apart from the railroad vine, the sprawling morning glory found on the lower reaches of the beach, several other species of morning glory may be seen on the dunes. The one known as the coastal morning glory is a trailing vine with deeply three-lobed leaves and a pink to purple funnel-shaped flower. There are several other low-growing plants. The dayflower, a widely distributed plant, has two blue petals and a third, smaller, whitish one, all of which generally wither before noon. Flowers appear singly each day or so within the folds of greenish bracts. Poor man's patch has a yellow flower. Its leaves and stems are covered with rigid, hooked hairs so that a passerby is often left with a leaf patch on his clothing. Tread softly, as its name implies, carries a threat. The plant is armed with many long, stiff, stinging hairs that can produce a painful rash. It has deeply three-lobed leaves and small, five-petalled white flowers.

Farther back on the dune is a sea grape, reduced by the winds to a stunted bush. Its big, round, rose-veined, leathery leaves and its edible, reddish purple fruits are common sights all along the seacoast. Here the vegetation becomes woodier and larger. It is the beginning of a coastal hammock with such shrubs and trees as cabbage palm, gumbo limbo, poisonwood, wild coffee, and white stopper.

6. ROCK REEF

At low tide a strip or ridge of rocks is exposed along many of the sandy beaches of south Florida. Most of this beach rock consists of soft limestone produced from the large quantities of calcium carbonate contained in the warm sea waters. (Different conditions exist on the Keys. There the rocky shores are exposed, eroded limestone, not formations on beaches.) Much of these rock formations is subjected to the constant erosion of the surf, so that the landscape is often in a state of transition. Greater stability exists in those areas where the rock outcroppings are protected by an offshore bar or coral reef. Part of the change that is constantly taking place is caused by the animals that inhabit this region. Some of these animals contribute to the breakdown, while others help in the buildup.

Most of the life in the rock reef is divided into zones. These zones are more or less determined by the turbidity of the waves, the changes of temperature, and the ability of an organism to survive exposure during low tide. The least hospitable zone is high up on the rocks, which is submerged for only a few hours a day and where sun, wind, and rain can quickly destroy a fragile animal. Survival depends upon the capacity to maintain a foothold and to conserve moisture. The chiton, the limpet, and the barnacle are among those qualified. The chiton is a small, primitive mollusk whose oval body is covered with an armorlike shell consisting of eight overlapping plates. A sluggish animal, it prefers to feed at night. During the day it stays firmly clamped to the rock, where its shell acts as an impenetrable shelter. The limpet, also a night-feeding mollusk, has a flat, disk-shaped shell. Unless taken unawares and pushed quickly aside, it is difficult to dislodge. Some species of limpet make a watertight seal by adjusting their shells into a depression that they and their predecessors have cut in the rock. The limpet returns to this position throughout its life.

The barnacle, which looks like a mollusk, is in fact a crustacean. Its life history is bizarre. The young barnacle in no way resembles the adult. In its larval stage, it is a free-swimming form that moults several times. When it is ready to settle down, it attaches its front end to the object it selects and makes its hold secure by secreting a cement that permanently fastens it to the spot. It then undergoes metamorphosis, obtaining a new shell covering and curled feathery legs. These feathery legs are used to sweep oxygen, plankton, and detritus from the water into its mouth. When falling tide exposes the barnacle to the air, it closes the valves at the top of its shell to form a cozy, protected chamber.

The barnacle has been picturesquely described as a crustacean

Brown Pelican

Nerites

Mermaid's Hair

Rock Crab

Sea Lettuce

Rock Shell

Periwinkles

Sergeant Major

Goby

Limpet

Honeycomb Rock

Padina (Peacock's Tail)

Halimeda

Chitons

Caulerpa

Anemone

Rock Barnacles

Honeycomb Worm (*Sabellaria*)

Hermit Crab

Ceriths

Whelk

Alive

Sea Urchin

Dead

Rock Reef

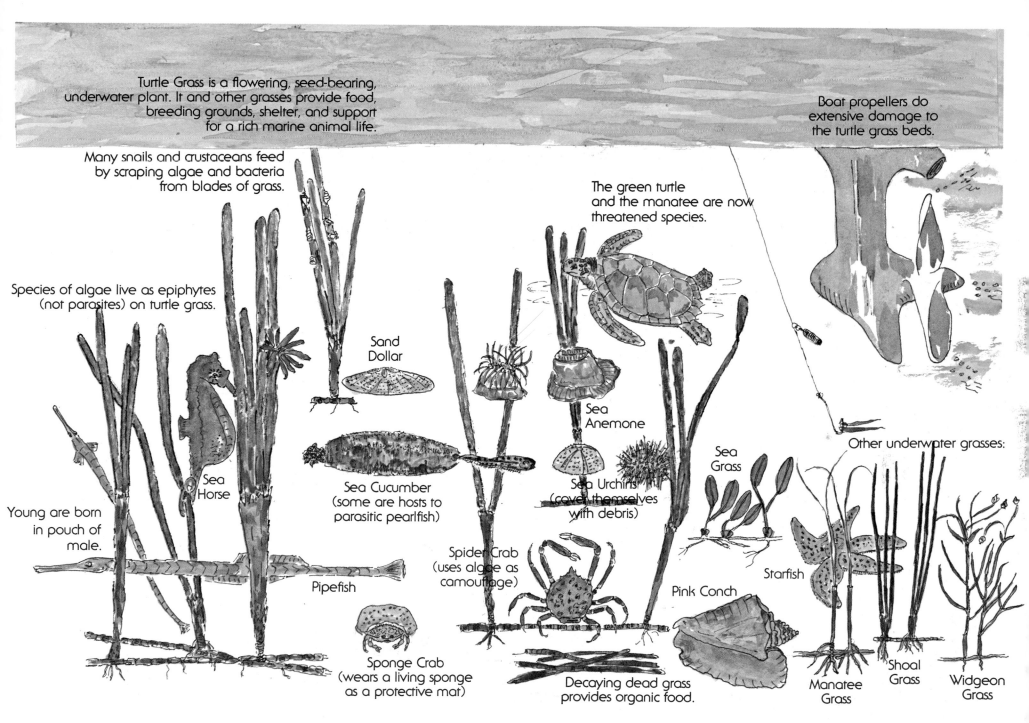

Turtle Grass is a flowering, seed-bearing, underwater plant. It and other grasses provide food, breeding grounds, shelter, and support for a rich marine animal life.

Boat propellers do extensive damage to the turtle grass beds.

Many snails and crustaceans feed by scraping algae and bacteria from blades of grass.

The green turtle and the manatee are now threatened species.

Species of algae live as epiphytes (not parasites) on turtle grass.

Sand Dollar

Sea Anemone

Other underwater grasses:

Sea Horse

Sea Grass

Young are born in pouch of male.

Sea Cucumber (some are hosts to parasitic pearlfish)

Sea Urchins (cover themselves with debris)

Starfish

Pipefish

Spider Crab (uses algae as camouflage)

Pink Conch

Sponge Crab (wears a living sponge as a protective mat)

Decaying dead grass provides organic food.

Manatee Grass

Shoal Grass

Widgeon Grass

Turtle Grass Jungle

standing permanently on its head and kicking food into its mouth with its legs. There are three broad classifications of barnacles. Acorn barnacles usually attach their shells directly to rocks, bridge pilings, wharves, and other stationary objects. They often whiten the object with a complete incrustation of shells. The genus known as goose barnacles has a long, flexible, fleshy stalk, generally only half an inch long. They attach their stalks mainly to logs and other floating debris. Since they cannot withstand strong currents, they are not common in areas where waves break against the rocks. The name goose barnacle is the product of a mistaken belief, which lasted for several centuries, that geese were hatched from these egg-shaped shells. The barnacles in the third class are parasitic animals, a species in this class infests the whale.

Another mollusk often found in the tidal regions of a rocky shore is the edible snail known as the periwinkle. Periwinkles live throughout the world, and, although all live in the coastal zone, different species inhabit different areas depending upon their respective abilities to withstand exposure to air. These distinct living zones prevent excessive competition among the various species. Because many actually live above the high tide line and can survive for long periods out of water, some biologists speculate that some species are moving toward a terrestrial condition. Evidence does indicate that many present-day land mollusks were at one time marine species, so the thought that some periwinkles are in the process of substituting a lung for a gill is no startling speculation. Periwinkles feed by scraping algae and detritus from the surface of rocks with their filelike tongues. In moving about they leave a trail of mucus. When living conditions become unfavorable, they preserve their moisture and exude pollutants by closing the operculum, colloquially known as the "trap door." Another common snail that is often found clinging to the upper regions of wave-washed rocks is the tropical nerites. The species known as bleeding teeth has white teethlike sections surrounded by an orange blotch.

Lower tidal regions of the rock formations provide a viable habitat for the less rugged animals. Here the retreating tides leave behind small pools that vibrate with activity as the offshore water rolls in and out of the dark caves and passages of the reef. While these tidal pools provide a place of refuge for animals and plants that cannot survive exposure even during periods of the lowest tides, there are other unique living problems. Especially in the calm waters of the South, a small pool exposed to the hot sun may in a short time reach an intolerably high temperature as compared to the temperature of the sea. The heat may also drive off some of the essential oxygen in the water and by causing excessive evaporation may increase the salinity of the pool to unbear-able limits. A quick summer shower, on the other hand, may dilute the salt content, causing equally destructive consequences.

Despite these possible adverse conditions, life in the tide pool presents a colorful, varied, and fascinating panorama. Many species of algae, known as seaweeds, hang from the shelves and sides of the rocks and cover much of the bottom. Seaweeds have no true leaves or stems and do not produce flowers. The vegetative body is called a frond. What corresponds to the root of a flowering plant is in seaweed a disk or expansion of the base. This is the holdfast, the means by which the frond attaches itself to a submerged body. Most of the seaweeds defend themselves against the force of the waves by simply swaying back and forth from a fixed position as the water rushes by.

The variety of the shapes, textures, and colors of the seaweeds is fascinating. One of the most common of these plants is the thin, silky, brilliant-green sea lettuce. One of the most beautiful is the peacock's tail. Its frond is leathery, fan-shaped, deeply cleft, and flares out like a skirt. The *Halimeda* resembles a series of green plates strung together like jewelry. The green, hairlike algae is known as mermaid's hair. The *Caulerpa* hangs down from the rock ledge like a compact mass of small, elongated, translucent green grapes. Among these and the other species of seaweed is the miniature underwater world of marine life, where small fishes, snails, starfish, sea urchins, sea anemones, shrimp, crabs, worms, sponges, jellyfishes, and octopi interact with one another.

Fairly common fishes in the tide pools are the small gobies and blennies. Both are poor swimmers and spend a good part of the time almost motionless on the bottom of the pool. They move suddenly only to gulp at a passing worm or shrimp. Some jump from one tide pool to another in search of better living conditions. The goby has a special formation of fins on its undersurface. This acts as a suction disk with which the goby can cling to firm surfaces when tidal waves become too powerful. Small crabs scurry across the rocks scavenging for scraps of food. Sea urchins move about slowly on distended tube feet that project beyond their spines. The shells, or tests, of dead urchins are often washed up on the beach. The principal enemy of the sea urchin is the starfish, which moves along in a gliding motion and which can regain by natural growth parts of the body that are lost. Sea anemones are armed with stinging cells with which they can capture their food, mainly small worms and crustaceans. They themselves are highly sensitive and at the first sign of a threat quickly change from beautiful flowerlike shapes to unattractive, tight masses. They are colonial animals and in their green, blue, or brown colors form extensive carpets in the rock cavities.

Additional spectacles in the underwater scene are supplied by sponges of all colors, by a variety of multicolored seashells, by the brilliant stripes and spots of tropical fishes, by the scuttling movements of hermit crabs carrying homes of snail shells, and by the beautiful tentacles of tube-building worms. The whole is a scene of endless feeding by a multitude of diverse plants and animals.

Various types of tube-building worms are often found attached to rocks and to shells of mollusks. The different species have characteristic tubes. One of the most interesting of these tube-building worms is the *Sabellaria*, generally known as the honeycomb worm. Starting with some solid object in low tidal regions, each worm constructs a tube by cementing together grains of sand with a mucuslike secretion. In time an active colony can build a mass of interlaced shells that gradually keeps enlarging until it has the appearance of an immense honeycomb. Each worm has plumelike gills attached to the front of its body, secure in its own tube, it depends on the action of the waves to furnish it a supply of food and building material. Vacant tubes become filled with sand and silt, and new tubes are attached to older ones. The final result is a large porous structure that can extend as a solid barrier across the beach for many yards and that appears to withstand the pounding of the waves just as effectively as the rock reef itself.

7. TURTLE GRASS JUNGLE

In some of the regions along the lower east and west coasts of Florida much of the debris cast up by the tide is masses of long, narrow blades of grass. This is the waste matter of the vast underwater fields that occur in the shallower waters of bays and beaches. The depth of the water in these areas is generally from four to eight feet, and some sections are exposed as mud flats at low tide. Several species of flowering plants occur in these underwater meadows. The most abundant vegetation is turtle grass, so named because it is a food of the green sea turtle.

Most marine plants are seaweeds, the simplest form of vegetation. Turtle grass, like the northern eelgrass, is an exception. It is a true flowering underwater plant that developed on land and then retreated to the sea. It has roots and leaves and produces flowers and seeds. Its leaves are straplike, about one-half inch wide and one to two feet long. Its flower blooms underwater, and its fruit produces seeds that take root and propagate in the shallow bottoms. Since turtle grass must rely on sunlight for growth, its depth depends in part on the clarity of the water in which it is growing. It also multiplies by sprouting new leaves from its underground stems.

Several other grasses are often found in association with turtle grass. These include shoal grass (narrow flat leaves with three-pointed tips); manatee grass (thin round leaves with blunt tips); widgeon grass (thin leaves in bushy clusters); and sea grass (long-stalked limp leaves in pairs, with conspicuous midvein). In the shallow and sheltered waters in which these plants grow, thousands upon thousands of thin blades of turtle grass, rising close to the surface, sway gently with the tidal currents and form a protective and nutritious jungle for the crowded population of organisms that inhabit this region. Attached to the blades of grass, very small, often microscopic, plants and animals find food and shelter. Worms, crabs, snails, and clams thrive in the muddy or sandy bottoms, rich with dead leaves and decaying roots. Filter-feeding animals devour part of the detritus, and bacteria break down some of it into rich chemical fertilizer. The food supply is abundant and varied, with as many as 100 different species of algae living as epiphytes on the blades of grass. The grass itself is food for some fishes and for countless small invertebrates. All of this ecological community is held together by the roots of the plants, which stabilize the bay bottoms by keeping the sediment firmly in place. The water surface appears placid, but beneath the surface is a feverish, interdependent, and productive marine environment providing much of the nourishment for many forms of life in the coastal areas.

For many years, the turtle grass beds were the feeding grounds and shelter areas for the manatee and the green turtle. Both of these animals are now threatened species, and neither plays a significant role in the sea grass communities. The manatee, or sea cow, is a plant-eating marine mammal that was overhunted for its meat, oil, and leather before it was given legal protection from this hazard. Today, the major threat to its limited population is the propeller of a speeding motorboat or a powerful barge. Because of the manatee's capacity to consume large quantities of aquatic vegetation, some marine scientists are exploring the possibility of using these animals in a weed-control program to clear noxious plants from clogged Florida waterways. The problems of breeding and maintaining a large enough herd for this purpose, and related problems of harboring the animals in colder weather, are fairly formidable, so that the ultimate survival of the species seems to depend

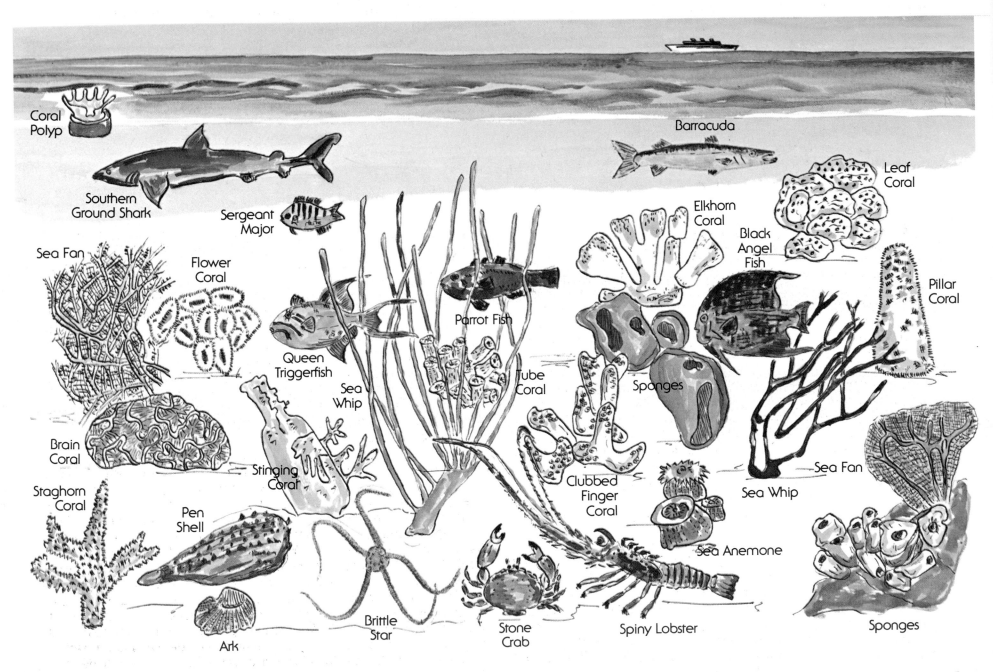

Coral Reef

in large part on the boater's willingness to slow down while in the habitat of the manatee. Even the grass beds themselves are sometimes victimized by the speed boats. Swaths of vegetation cut out by churning propellers become enlarged by tidal action. This is the first stage in the piecemeal destruction of the environment.

The green turtle, like the manatee, is one of the few large animals that feeds directly on sea grasses. At the breeding season the turtles must swim to shore where the females lay their eggs in the sand. The demand for these eggs and the ease with which man can capture the turtles for their tasty meat have made their future uncertain.

Much of life in the turtle grass flats depends on the art of concealment and camouflage. The pipefishes are almost invisible as they hover upright in the sea grass environment, resembling the flat blades of grass. With them are the sea horses, who drift, heads up and tails down, mimicking the vegetation, or are coiled almost motionless around blades of grass. Both of these animals belong to the order of tube-mouthed fishes, which capture their prey by sucking water through their elongated snouts. Pipefishes and seahorses are especially interesting because of their curious method of reproduction. Females lay their eggs in the brood pouches of the male, where the eggs incubate until the young are born alive. Very few species of animals assign the hatchery function to the males.

Some of the other animals, especially those that have sluggish habits, are even more skillful at making themselves appear part of the surroundings. Although sea urchins are well protected by spines and have few enemies after maturity, they live lazily in secluded places, and for further concealment disguise themselves with bits of seaweed, shell, and other debris. Spider crabs are often covered with seaweeds, corals, and other organisms, which they gather with their long, flexible legs and place upon their backs to hide from their predators. The coats of these crabs are covered with hooked and serrated hairs that aid in holding the transplanted organisms in place. The sponge crab wears a living sponge as a protective shield. The crab breaks off a suitable piece of sponge, hollows out part of it, and uses its hind legs, which are bent over its back, to hold the sponge in position. Since the sponge contains hundreds of small bonelike particles, few animals threaten the crab. Another curious little spider crab uses its hind legs to carry half a shell over its back.

The grass beds are home for a great many other animals. The patches of vegetation offer shelter to a variety of sea shells, including tulip shells, conchs, pens, cockles, and murexes. The sea hare, a large-sized snail with no external shell, swims slowly through the grass beds by rippling its wide, winglike fins. It repels its attackers by ejecting a cloud of poisonous fluid. In addition to the sea urchins, the spiny-skinned animals include sea stars, sand dollars, and sea cucumbers. The most abundant of these is the sea cucumber, which bears little resemblance to the other members of its group because it has a so-called head and tail, instead of a radially symmetrical structure. When confronted by a predator, the sea cucumber throws out its internal organs and in the process discharges a defensive poison. Like the ability of sea stars to regenerate lost arms, the sea cucumber can regrow new organs. The sea cucumber has a unique relationship with the parasitic pearlfish that lives inside the body of the cucumber, sometimes feeding on the cucumber's tissues and sometimes leaving its host to feed on the outside.

The importance of these grassy flats was not fully appreciated until the eelgrass along the North Atlantic coast was destroyed some years ago by a mysterious plague. Soon thereafter life in the bays decreased. Species of minute plants and animals that lived on the blades of grass vanished. The supply of detritus from decayed plant material dwindled. Fewer fish were caught, beds of mussel diminished, and scallops became rarities. Only when the eelgrass reestablished itself did life in the bays begin to return to its former opulence. Turtle grass performs the same functions in the South as eelgrass does in the North. Destruction of these beds by propeller-slashing, pollution, filling, or dredging strikes an outrageous blow at an important biological community.

8. CORAL REEF

Most of the living corals in the continental United States exist and flourish in a shallow, limestone shelf that was once the bottom of the sea that covered southern Florida. This coral reef is about four miles wide and runs parallel to the Florida Keys, a few miles offshore. This area satisfies the need of reef-building corals for warm, clear, salty water.

Reef corals are delicate animals. Water temperatures below 60 degrees Fahrenheit, the encroachment of sand or silt on their territory, or an increase or decrease in the normal salinity of seawater is fatal. Apart from these critical factors, vigorous coral growth requires exposure to water currents or wave action that will bring food to these immovable animals. Corals will not grow in deeper waters where currents and wave action are minimal and where the sunlight necessary for their growth cannot penetrate.

The corals sold in souvenir stores are merely the bleached skeletons of coral colonies. The hard, stony surface of these skeletons is lined with small cavities each of which was once occupied by a living polyp. Living polyps cover their skeletons with what feels like a soft, slimy skin. Polyps fall into the major group of invertebrates known as coelenterates, which includes such examples as sea anemones, jellyfishes, and Portuguese men-of-war. Coral polyps are carnivorous animals that feed upon minute planktonic organisms.

The polyp itself has a soft, hollow, tubular body with a mouth opening surrounded by numerous stinging tentacles. During the daytime these tentacles are withdrawn, but at night they lash out to paralyze passing prey and transfer it onto the mouth of the polyp. Reef-building corals contain within their tissues numerous blue-green algae, single-celled plants known as zooxanthellae. These tiny plants are necessary to the corals for optimum growth because they take in carbon dioxide from their surroundings and give off oxygen utilized by the polyps in their tissues for breathing. In exchange the plants use the carbon dioxide and other waste products given off by the polyps. This relationship is mutually beneficial to plant and animal, but because the plant needs sunlight for photosynthesis reef corals cannot live in deep water. Corals thrive best in depths from the 30-foot zone up to the surface of the water.

The hard skeletons produced by the soft living tissues of the polyps differentiate the coral from other coelenterates. The coral polyp protects its soft body by depositing a limestone cup around it, in much the same way as does an oyster. A coral colony begins when a fertilized egg produces a coral larva which after a free-swimming stage reaches a suitable hard surface and secretes a cementing substance that anchors the larva permanently to its home. The larva becomes a polyp, and its skin begins to build a stony skeleton. Coral polyps develop in a variety of ways—by growth of the individual polyp in size and complexity or by branching or budding. In the end large masses of limestone rock are produced in the form of coral reefs.

Thousands of species of plants and animals may contribute to the construction of a coral reef. By far the largest contributors to the structure are the coral polyps. Once the polyps establish themselves on a platform they begin their development as colonies. As these colonies grow upward and outward, each polyp deposits limestone around its body while it remains on the outside of the increasing mass. The interior of the mass is the limestone continually being laid down by the polyps. As the masses grow larger, they get closer together. Some colonies die.

Environmental requirements may deteriorate. Sediments or rubble may pile up to smother them. Borers and predator fish may attack them. New colonies begin to develop on the dead colonies or between the older colonies. In this way the reef grows upward toward the surface. As this process is going on, the spaces between the dead and live colonies become filled with enormous quantities of debris from the shells, bodies, and skeletons of calcareous organisms. In time all these elements may become solidified into a solid rock reef consisting of living coral colonies cemented together in a limestone foundation.

About 50 species of stony corals live in the Florida reef tract. The colonies of each species vary in size and shape. Some colonies branch out into treelike shapes with either thin, delicate branches or thick, massive limbs. Some form convoluted boulders. Others are platelike forms with short branches, and still others are delicate, lacy clusters. The sizes vary substantially from a few inches across to heights and diameters from eight to ten feet. In the deeper, more active waters, two of the most beautiful and prominent reef builders are the broad-branched elkhorn coral and its more delicate relative, the staghorn coral. Though both have long branches and are therefore easily broken at the tips, they form dense forestlike growths covering extensive areas. Another sturdy species is the less common pillar or cathedral coral that grows in thick columns, either singly or in branching stalks. Species of brain coral, whose structural form resembles the meandering grooves of the human brain, share the quieter water areas with the massive boulder types of the abundant star coral. In the shallow, relatively quiet waters, where some sediment is present, the smaller sized corals, varieties of finger and flower corals, form small but numerous colonies. "Stinging coral," so named because its cells can produce a severe welt when touched, looks like a true coral but is not closely related. It often grows in the form of an encrustation on other objects in the reef.

Some of the more colorful and conspicuous contributors to the limestone of the coral reef are the gorgonians—the sea whips, sea fans, and sea plumes. These "soft corals" have a flexible skeletal structure that sways with the movements of the water currents. Though they belong to the same class as hard corals, their polyps have eight tentacles, while the stony polyps have six or a multiple of six tentacles. In addition, they have a common digestive system that feeds the entire colony, whereas stony corals have individual stomachs. Soft corals add another dimension to the reef and contribute a special brilliance to the underwater pageant.

Thousands of species of plants and animals all live jumbled

Red Mangrove

Seedling (germinates on tree)

Black Mangrove

White Mangrove

Buttonwood

Raccoon

Land Crab

Red Mangrove Water Snake

Pneumatophores

Shrimp

Coon Oysters

Mangrove Shoots

Hog Snapper

Tarpon

Prop Roots

Menhaden

Mangrove Snapper

Blue Crab

Brown water stain

Snook

Mullet

Mangrove Miracle

together on a coral reef. Among the hundreds of fishes associated with the coral reef are the spectacular, glistening triggerfish, parrot fish, angel fish, and the little damselfish known as sergeant major. Triggerfishes bite off the tips of growing coral. Parrot fishes nibble on the coral and graze on the algae covering the limestone. The larger, less brilliant fishes include the groupers, barracudas, southern ground sharks, and the dangerous moray eels. There are small snapping shrimps, camouflaged spider crabs, and numerous larger crabs. Edible spiny lobsters and edible stone crabs hide in rock crevices or under small ledges. Parts of the limestone are riddled by boring sea worms, chiselled by sea urchins, and disintegrated by encrusting sponges. Many other sponges abound in a variety of shapes, sizes, and colors. The mollusks are well represented by such univalves as conchs, olive shells, and cowries, and such bivalves as arks, clams, pens, and oysters. Add to all these plume worms, sea anemones, squid, octopi, brittle stars, stingrays, turtles, and the abundant plant life that is the primary food source for the entire complex community, and there may be as many as 3,000 species. All contribute in one form or another to a balanced association of living organisms that has been flourishing for millions of years.

9. MANGROVE MIRACLE

Mangrove forests are spread over the coastal area of Florida from Cape Canaveral on the Atlantic, down around the southern portion of the peninsula, and up to the Cedar Key on the Gulf of Mexico. The mangroves that cover the southwestern shore of the state, especially the Ten Thousand Islands, make up one of the largest and most luxuriant mangrove forests in the world. The basic vegetation in these forests consists of four species of trees, three of which are loosely called mangroves, and a fourth that shares with the mangroves a preference for the habitat known as the estuary—the region where freshwater from the land reaches and mixes with the saltwater of the sea. Although they are sometimes found growing together, each of these trees frequently occupies a separate zone in this brackish environment. Other plants not resistant to salt offer no threat to the salt-defiant mangroves. Smaller plant species that are dependent upon sunlight are crowded out by the shade of the mangroves. The mangroves dominate the landscape.

The most spectacular of the trees is the red mangrove. It grows closest to the water's edge and is generally inundated at high tide. Its tall, arching, stiltlike roots, often covered with coon oysters, hold the body of the tree firmly in the unstable ground. Material washed down from the land or carried in by the tides is trapped in the thicket formed by these tangled prop roots, is slowly colonized by new vegetation, and in time often builds up into new land. While this land building process is going on, the red mangrove keeps marching farther out into the sea. This process occurs because of an ingenious reproductive device. Before a seed drops from its parent tree, it first germinates into a partially rooted, cigar-shaped seedling. When the seedling falls it may take root in the forest floor beneath the tree. Or, it may drift in the sea with tides and currents and ultimately take root in some distant mud flat that has been left exposed by an exceptionally low tide. If it survives some later storm, it will begin on its own an island building process with the silt, vegetation, shells, driftwood, and other debris that become entrapped in its tangled roots.

Closer to the shore, the black mangrove and the white mangrove both contribute to the land building process. The black mangroves can be quickly recognized by the hundreds of breathing tubes, called pneumatophores, which stick up out of the mud like small, pencil-thin militiamen. The upright projections provide regular aeration for the mass of underground roots. Although the white mangrove has no outstanding visible characteristic, its root system also catches and holds some of the available debris. The bottom side of the leaf of both the white and black mangrove is often coated with salt crystals—the residue of the process of taking in and excreting salt. Farther inland, on ground flooded only by the highest tides, is the fourth member of these salt-tolerant species—the buttonwood. It derives its name from its small, round fruits that resemble old-fashioned shoe buttons. It also contributes to the debris-collecting process by sending up straight shoots from trunks that have been knocked over by storms.

Together, these four species of trees dominate the estuaries where organic material washed down from the marshes mixes with decaying plant material to make one of the most productive natural areas on earth. Here, in these shoreline forests, often called wastelands by some, a remarkably rich and varied food web supports an environment teeming with marine life. The food chain begins with decaying mangrove leaves colonized by microorganisms, which are grazed upon by one-celled animals, which are in turn eaten by tiny invertebrates, such as shrimp, worms, and small crabs, which then become food for larger invertebrates and a variety of small fishes, such as young snook, tarpon, menhaden, hog snapper, and mangrove snapper. The small fishes are eaten by the big fishes, which are eaten by bigger fishes, which ultimately are often caught and eaten by man. Along the way other fish eaters intervene; for example, the wading birds, the eagles, the ospreys, the vultures, and the alligators.

Shrimp play an important part in many of the marine food chains. Shrimp spawn offshore near the islands of the Dry Tortugas, and the young move into the estuaries on the spring flood tides. This is just at the time when the combination of rains and tides bring in a rich food supply. Although shrimp eaters may be around, the estuaries are still a much safer nursery ground than the predator-infested open sea. By fall the shrimp are nearly mature. On the high tides of the autumn equinox they begin the move back to the shrimp beds of the Tortugas, where large catches are harvested annually by commercial fishermen. The shrimp are not alone in their movements. Blue crab, snook, tarpon, bass, sea trout, and many other important fish adjust their life cycles so they can zero in on the protection and food supply of the estuaries—a food supply that does not require plowing, cultivating, or fertilizing. All it needs is to be left alone.

The mangrove forests stand firm on the shorelines of Florida as guardians of the mainland, ready to absorb the sweep of tidal waters and the blast of stormy winds. They are tough environments, with seasonal changes in temperature, salinity, oxygen, and turbidity. They offer generous food supplies and protected habitats to those birds, reptiles, crustaceans, mollusks, and fishes that can adjust to the stresses and limitations of the mangroves. Their dense, umbrella-shaped crowns of dark green foliage provide nesting places for colonies of herons, ibises, and other wading birds. These forests represent a great natural resource that plays an essential role in the whole ecology of the seas.

10. WADING BIRDS

Southern Florida has long been known for its bird life. The large water birds claim the most attention. The variety and abundance of wading birds in the shallow ponds, bays, lagoons, and swamps is truly spectacular. During the summer and fall, when water is plentiful, these showy birds are scattered over the wide ranges of the Everglades. When the winter drought sets in and the large inland sloughs dry up, then the small fishes and other aquatic life on which these birds feed become densely concentrated in the more permanent pools along the coast. It is here in the mangrove islands, cypress forests, and other trees where many of the wading birds establish their mixed rookeries.

There is little doubt that most wading birds agree upon the basic specifications for a good nesting site: a heavy supply of available food, essential for satisfying the enormous appetites of their fledglings; clusters of trees that will support their nests; a good supply of twigs and other nest-building materials; and relative safety from raccoons, rats, snakes, and other terrestrial predators. The ability and willingness of these birds to fraternize is evidenced also in the way they share a common food supply. Many of them can feed together in the same pond in a variety of feeding methods. Their physical characteristics and habits relegate each species to a separate niche in the general community.

Standing statuesquely tall, knee-deep in either salt or freshwater, is the great blue heron, one of the most common of the herons. Its white head, with the black crest stretching out behind, tops the uniform slate blue of its large body. Stately and slow moving, it often stands motionless, sometimes with one leg raised, watching for the telltale ripple of a fish, shrimp, or other prey, and then strikes with unerring accuracy. It can swallow a fish weighing as much as a pound and any of the water snakes. It begins its flight by spreading magnificent great wings and then sails away effortlessly.

The distinguishing features of the American or common egret are its yellow bill and black legs. Though smaller than the great blue, it has

Yellow-crowned
Night Heron

Black-crowned
Night Heron

Glossy Ibis

Wood Stork
(in flight)

Wood
Stork

White
Ibis

Great
Blue Heron

Little
Blue Heron

Least
Bittern

Reddish Egret
(canopy feeding)

Snowy Egret
(display)

American
Bittern

Louisiana
Heron

Roseate
Spoonbill

Green Heron

Common
Egret

Wading Birds

Willet

Black-necked Stilt

Short-billed Dowitcher

Black Skimmer

Rudy Turnstone

Plovers:

Wilson's

Marbled Godwit

Knot

Black-bellied Plover

Semipalmated

Piping

Whimbril

Florida Crown Conch

Dunlin

Killifish

Western Sandpiper

Fargo's Worm Shell

Banded Tulip

Fiddler Crab

Plumed Worm

Tidal Mud Flat

many of the latter's feeding techniques. It too moves slowly and deliberately, holding its head immobile, stalking the prey until it is ready to strike.

Another stalking water bird, which along with the American egret was a victim of the notorious plume hunters, is the smaller snowy egret. It has a black bill, black legs, and yellow feet, and as it steps gingerly through the shadows it lifts its "golden slipper" daintily out of the water with each deliberate step. During the mating and nesting seasons, the snowy will greet his mate and his young with a courtly display of open wings and a raised crest.

Another common heron is the Louisiana heron, a dark bird with snowy white underparts, that runs through the shallow saltwater flats in the hope of stirring up its prey. Occasionally, it will venture into deepr water, fishing with outstretched neck close to the surface.

The most active of the waders is the uncommon reddish egret of the saltwater flats. Unlike other herons, it runs, lurches, stumbles, and dashes to the left and right in a comic pursuit of its quarry. It spreads its wings in canopy fashion, creating a shadow in which frightened fish and other small animals mistakenly seek shelter. There they become easy victims.

A spectacular wading bird is the roseate spoonbill. An adult spoonbill has bright pink feathers and wings, red legs and red eyes, and a unique bill—long and flattened and with a spoon-shaped tip. It wades in shallow water, swinging its bill back and forth and filling it with the bottom debris. Out of this it screens and swallows the living organisms, allowing the mud and other inorganic matter to drain from its broad mandible.

The strangest of the wading birds is the wood stork, sometimes called the wood ibis. It is a large white bird with black feathers on its wings and tail, standing almost as tall as the great blue heron. Its bill is long, very thick, and scythe shaped, its legs are long and meatless, and its head is a bald dark knob. It feeds by groping steadily through shallow waters, probing and disturbing the muddy bottom and snapping its partly open beak when it makes contact with a fish. It is an ungainly bird on the ground, but in flight, with neck and legs extended and with wing beats slow and powerful, it makes an eye-catching wildlife spectacle.

The feeding habits of the white ibis are similar to those of the stork. It is a smaller bird with a red face, red legs, and a thin, decurved red bill. They are often seen in long, wavy flight patterns, the small black wing tips plainly visible, as they converge on mangrove islands and slowly circle to locate a resting place for the night. Except for its uniform brown-bronze color, the less common glossy ibis resembles the white. Both feed extensively on crayfish obtained in the soft marshy areas.

The smaller birds congregate in the more shallow areas and among the protective vegetation. The little blue heron wades slowly along the pond margins, tilting his head from side to side for a better view of his prey. The roll call of herons includes the green heron, two night herons, and two species of bitterns. The "little" green heron, too short-legged to wade, fishes either from the shore or while perched on low mangrove roots. The two night herons have heavy bodies and short thick necks: the black-crowned roosts in trees during the day and hunts at night; the slimmer yellow-crowned, also a night prowler, can sometimes be seen during the daytime poking among the thickets. The American bittern, with its speckled brown feathers, becomes very elusive, particularly when it freezes in position among the grasses and sedges of its freshwater marshy home. The smallest of the herons, the least bittern, is a weak flier. It, too, seeks the safety of camouflage by freezing in the tall, freshwater vegetation.

Despite the abundance of the wading birds, many of them are constantly in danger. Plume-hunting days are over, but new pressures exist. Among the threats are the dredging of the marshes, the reclaiming of land from the tidal channels, the alteration of the natural flow of freshwater, and, of course, the presence of pesticides. For the present, however, the life of the wading birds is an unfailing source of beauty and interest for the observer.

11. TIDAL MUD FLAT

All along the eastern coast of the United States, from Maine to the tip of Florida and up around its western shore, is a strip of soft, salty, wet, low-lying land. This continuous green ribbon of salt marshes is broken only by the great estuaries and rivers that flow into the ocean. It is a harsh and hostile environment for land plants in which the number of species is limited by the requirement that roots and leaves survive in constant contact with salty water.

For animals, however, the mud in the tidal flats offers a more hospitable environment. Its appearance is dirty and forbidding, and its smell is offensive, but it is packed with rich deposits of organic debris that support an intimate burrowing population in prodigious numbers. The slimy mud is easily penetrated by soft-bodied creatures, and the blanket of mud provides a stable and protective environment. The variety of marine worms is large: trumpet worms in their sandy cases, plumed worms in parchmentlike tubes, and lug worms that grow long and stout in the mud. Buried alongside the worms are ark clams, cockles, tellins, corrugated razor clams, and worm shells. Univalves are plentiful, including the banded tulip, the Florida fighting conch, and a variety of small mud snails. Ghost shrimp, snapping shrimp, mud crabs, and other crustaceans burrow into the mud. Along the surface of the mud there are beach fleas, sand hoppers, and aquatic insects.

When the tide rises the warm, shallow waters bristle with activity. Fish and crabs swim or walk in with the tide to eat any animals that have carelessly moved outside their burrows. Small blue crabs that have hidden in the mud come out to swim and search for food. The tide pools shimmer as the small fish dart from one side to the other. There are the mummichogs, the banded killifish, and the minnow known as *Gambusia*. This minnow bears its young alive and makes mosquito larvae its principal food. Some of the water animals leave when the tide recedes, but the pools trapped by low tides still teem with large colonies.

At low tide the mud flats are filled with shorebirds, feeding on the rich nutrients and abundant animal life and resting in the open areas. Some of the birds are close relatives of inland species: red-winged blackbirds and marsh wrens. But most of the birds have adapted specifically to fill their roles in the world of the saltwater flat. Some nest in the luxurious crowns of the mangrove forests. Others nest in the adjacent areas and use the mud flats as their primary feeding grounds. The long-legged wading birds of the heron family—so much a part of the mangrove habitats—can be seen here along with congregations of other shorebirds. Apart from the herons and their allies, the long-legged birds include the marbled godwit, the whimbrel, and the black-necked stilt. The marbled godwit has a long, turned-up bill and mottled brown plumage. The whimbrel, smaller than the marbled godwit, is recognized by the distinct striping on its crown, its pale underbody, and the long, downcurved bill that it uses to dig crustaceans, mollusks, and worms out of the mud. The long, thin neck, the black upper plumage, the red legs, and the thin, straight bill make the black-necked stilt stand out.

Among the medium-sized to smaller shorebirds are the plovers. Their necks and tails are short, and their short bills have noticeable swellings near the tip. The black-bellied (shown in winter plumage) is the largest of the plovers. The white rump and white-banded tail are its special field marks. There are several banded plovers. The piping plover has a single, broken neckband. The semipalmated has a prominent white collar and a single neckband. The neckband of the larger Wilson's plover is wider, and its bill is heavier. The killdeer, a noisy bird often seen in fields at a distance from the water, has two neckbands. Other medium-sized birds include the willet, which can be recognized in flight by its striking black and white wing pattern. Another is the rudy turnstone, which, like the plovers, uses its bill to turn up stones, seaweed, and shells in its search for food and which can be spotted by its conspicuous wing pattern of black, brown, and white.

A number of birds in the mud flats are known as sandpipers. The dunlin is stocky and short necked with a long, slightly downcurved bill. The knot is another short-necked, stocky bird, but with a short bill. The dowitchers have long bills that they pump up and down in the mud, like a sewing machine needle, in search of worms and larvae. The smallest of the sandpipers are the birds usually referred to as "peeps"—a term used to encompass several species. Many of the peeps are often seen along the shoreline. The most common in the mud flats is the western sandpiper.

Other birds are in flight above the watery areas. Some gulls may be seen floating overhead, moving from one feeding place to another. Terns dive headlong into the water in search of small fish and insects. There may be an osprey hovering at great heights or a hawk gliding a few feet above the ground. The spectacular black skimmer, commonly called "cutwater," may be seen in its unique feeding technique. Its specially constructed long, red bill tipped with black is a unique adaptation for life in the saltwater community. The lower mandible is longer than the upper. The bird flies along the top of the water, the lower mandible cutting the surface in a straight line. When contact is made with a fish feeding at the top of the water, the skimmer snaps its head down and completes the capture by closing its bill.

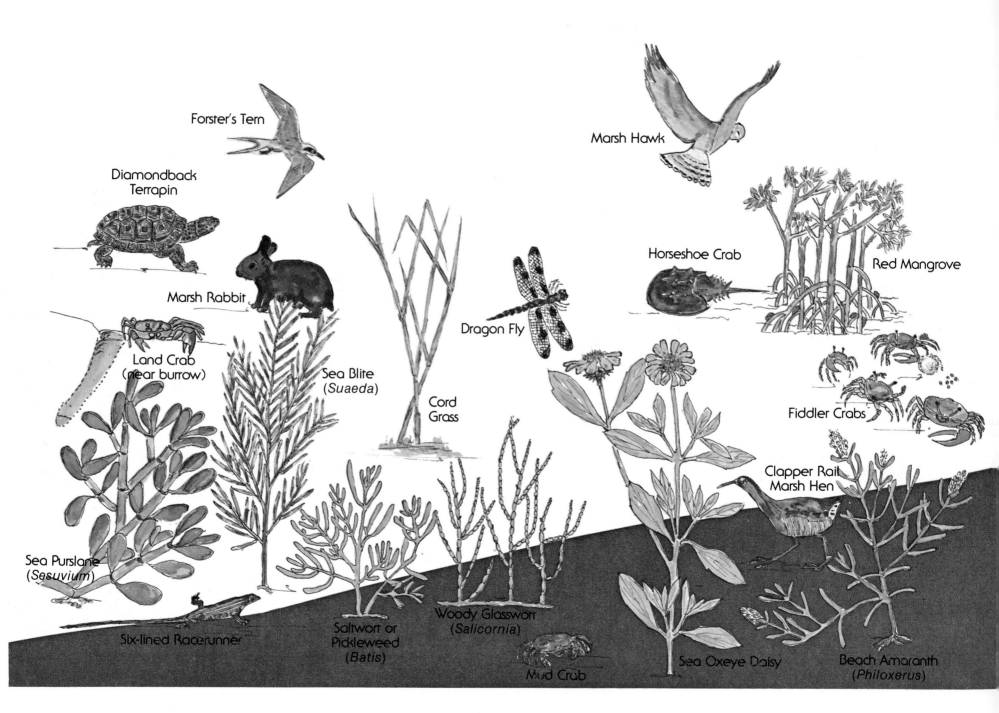

Forster's Tern

Diamondback
Terrapin

Marsh Hawk

Marsh Rabbit

Horseshoe Crab

Red Mangrove

Land Crab
(near burrow)

Sea Blite
(*Suaeda*)

Dragon Fly

Cord
Grass

Fiddler Crabs

Clapper Rail
Marsh Hen

Sea Purslane
(*Sesuvium*)

Six-lined Racerunner

Saltwort or
Pickleweed
(*Batis*)

Woody Glasswort
(*Salicornia*)

Mud Crab

Sea Oxeye Daisy

Beach Amaranth
(*Philoxerus*)

Salt Water Marsh

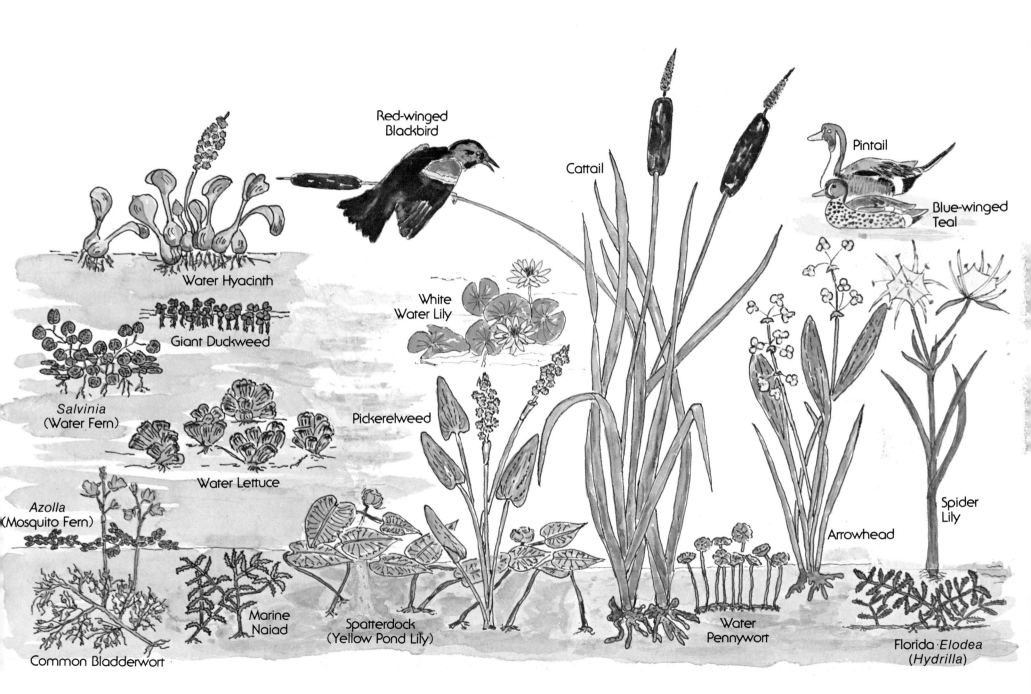

Red-winged Blackbird

Water Hyacinth

Giant Duckweed

Salvinia (Water Fern)

Water Lettuce

Azolla (Mosquito Fern)

Common Bladderwort

Marine Naiad

Spatterdock (Yellow Pond Lily)

White Water Lily

Pickerelweed

Cattail

Water Pennywort

Pintail

Blue-winged Teal

Arrowhead

Spider Lily

Florida *Elodea* (*Hydrilla*)

Freshwater Pond

On the landward edge of the mud flat is the saltwater marsh. This land is the intermediate area between the mud flat and the dry land. Many of the animals in the edge of this zone move freely in and out of the mud flats. Among these are the fiddler crab, the clapper rail, the diamondbacked terrapin, and the ubiquitous raccoon. A strange type of green vegetation marks the end of the tidal flats.

12. SALTWATER MARSHES

As the land rises from the sea, the tidal mud flat merges into a marshy salt meadow. This intermediate zone between mud and dry land provides a habitat for animals and plants that can withstand some salt, freshwater dilution during rains, and exposure to sun and air. The terrain is not particularly hospitable, and it produces a vegetation all its own.

Many of the animals here move freely back and forth from the mud flats. The seaward edge of the marsh is the domain of *Uca*, the fiddler crab. The males have one very large claw; the other is small. The large claw looks like a fiddle, the small one like a bow. This, together with the waving action of the large claw, accounts for their common name. Fiddler crabs congregate in herds and excavate their burrows above the mid-tide level. The depth of these burrows depends on the distance to moist, but not saturated, mud. At low tide they leave their cavities and swarm across the mud flats in search of food, wheeling and turning as a unit. At the first sign of danger they retreat, each scurrying into his own burrow. With the rising tide they move back. When flooding threatens, each descends into its home, plugs up the opening, and waits for the tide to recede. Fiddlers have developed a primitive lung, so that as long as the burrow is moist, this lung can serve for breathing air.

On the more elevated portions of the marsh, above the high-tide line, are the burrows of *Cardisoma*, the giant land crabs. These heavy-bodied crabs, often called square-backed crabs, have rectangular carapaces (shells) and short, stout eyestalks. Their burrows are large, sometimes extending three or four feet to the level of the water. Land crabs are capable of living great distances inland, but at spawning time there is a mass procession to the sea so that the females can liberate the young in salt water. The reverse procedure is followed by *Limulus*, the horseshoe crab, the last survivor of an ancient group of animals related to spiders and scorpions. These crabs live on muddy shores below the low watermark, but at breeding season they come ashore so that the female's eggs can be deposited near the high water line.

The plant that best characterizes the border between the mud flat and dry land is sea purslane (*Sesuvium*). It is a vinelike, perennial herb, with fleshy, spatula-shaped leaves that hug the sand as a ground cover. There are other salt-tolerant succulents that act as ground covers. Woody glasswort (*Salicornia virginica*), whose common name comes from the crunchy sound made when mats of this plant are walked upon, is also a perennial herb with a jointed stem and with leaves that have been reduced to small scales. Saltwort or pickleweed (*Batis maritima*) is a low, smooth shrub with narrow, curved, pale green leaves, that sprawls on the ground along with the woody glassworts. Beach amaranth (*Philoxerus vermicularis*) is a prostrate herb with creeping, six-foot branches, narrow leaves, and small, silvery-white flower spikes. Finally, sea blite (*Suaeda linearis*) is a tall herb, with many ascending stems. All these plants are edible if cooked, some can be eaten raw, and others are tasty if pickled. The oxeye daisy or the sea oxeye (*Borrichia*) is a fleshy herb that has whitish stems and leaves and yellow sunflowerlike blossoms. Here and there are occasional specimens of *Spartina*, the grass that dominates the marshes in the North.

The sounds of birds echo in the marshes. Of these the clapper rail or marsh hen is considered truly symbolic of the region. Its thin-as-a-rail shape permits it to thread through the vegetation elusively, barely disturbing the leaves in its pursuit of fiddler crabs. Its less-than-musical cackle can often be heard, but the bird itself is difficult to spot. The marsh hawk, gliding low above the ground, is in search of rodents. Forster's tern, rarely seen on the coastal beaches, is a common sight. In winter its orange bill becomes blackish and its black cap is reduced to an eyepatch.

Among the land animals is the diamondback terrapin, which has been taken for food in abundant numbers. Thousands of dragonflies display their gauzy wings. Raccoons and swamp rabbits invade the marsh from the landward side. The dark coloring and shorter ears distinguish the marsh rabbit from the well-known cottontail. The mammals are typical land dwellers and are driven onto higher ground with each high tide. The tide is vital to the salt marsh, as it is to the mud flat, and both are essential parts of the larger system where fresh and salt waters mix—a system that is economically, aesthetically, and scientifically valuable.

13. FRESHWATER POND

A pond is generally defined as a quiet, shallow body of water, much of which is covered with rooted vegetation. Its central open area distinguishes it from a marsh or a swamp. Life in a pond community is in a constant process of change. In its earliest stage decaying matter from plants and animals settle to the bottom of the pond. This stimulates the growth of algae. The algae become the basic foods for plant-eating animals, which in turn become food for flesh-eating animals. The soil and water become enriched. Plants begin to emerge from the edge of the pond. Various species of new plants begin to float and accumulate on the surface of the water. Underwater plants begin to develop and cover the bottom of the pond.

As the plant population increases and changes so does the animal life. More and more organic matter is added to the sediment of the pond as death and decay continue. The rooted plants begin to expand their coverage. Year after year, and decade after decade, the process continues and accelerates. Eventually, vegetation covers the whole area, and the pond has reached the stage of a marsh. The filling process continues. The process of succession is inexorable. Bushes and trees begin to encroach upon the marsh. The marsh becomes a swamp and the swamp becomes a forest, as nature's technique of land reclamation reaches its climax.

In many sections of Florida the drop in the water table, primarily the result of man-made drainage systems, has accelerated the process of succession. What were formerly ponds are now shallow depressions, frequently marked by cocoplum, buttonbush, saltbush, and other border plants. Pine trees have taken possession of the dry pond bottoms, and, barring invasion by exotic plants or major environmental changes, the steady transition to a climax forest has begun.

Despite the rapid impact of drainage, there are still numerous ponds in Florida, each a self-contained habitat, producing everything necessary for a balanced environment. The most conspicuous and most essential elements of this environment are the plants. These are generally classified on the basis of the zones in which they live: the floating plant zone, the emergent plant zone, the submergent plant zone, and the shoreline. The fifth zone is the open water area where life consists largely of turtles, birds, large fish, and small microscopic plants and animals that drift suspended in the pond. In late summer these suspended organisms occur in enormous abundance and when massed together look like golden green mats of floating moss. They collect around the stems and underwater parts of the various pond plants. This is the broad base on which the food pyramids in freshwater ponds are built.

A very common plant in the floating zone is the water hyacinth. This plant was introduced into Florida from South America and, because of its incredible rate of multiplication, has become a navigational hazard and a biological pest. Its swollen leafstalks give the plant its buoyancy. Its feathery roots provide a secure habitat for small animals, and its leaves and leafstalks are sometimes eaten by coots. Big dense colonies are common sights throughout the state. The presence of water hyacinths always indicates that the water has a large supply of fertilizer or nutrients.

Another floating plant frequently found in dense colonies is water lettuce. Its most notable characteristic is the light yellow green leaves in the form of a rosette. The leaves are spongy and inflated and have several distinct nerves radiating from the base. Its wildlife utilization value is quite poor. Still another floating plant that sometimes forms dense surface mats, especially in stagnant or sheltered ponds, is giant duckweed. The plant is green above, often reddish underneath. A cluster of roots dangles in the water from each plant. It has good wildlife value, the entire plant is usually consumed by coots and ducks.

Two of the floating plants are members of the water fern family. *Salvinia* grows best in shallow ponds, often in association with other aquatic vegetation. Its small, bright green leaf is distinctly midribbed, often appearing folded in the center. The other member of the water fern family is *Azolla*, sometimes called water velvets or mosquito fern. It is generally found on the periphery of ponds. Its small, individual leaves are banded together in a scalelike manner. The upper portion of each leaf is in the air and the lower portion is submersed. Both of the water ferns have only slight wildlife value.

The emergent plants are those that are rooted in the soil and grow through the water. These are the most striking plants in the pond. The tallest is the cattail, with leaves that are often seven feet high. The flowers are in a cylindrical spike; the brown, dense lower portion is the female flower, and the upper portion is the male flower. While the wildlife value of the cattail is generally negligible except for providing a place for fowl roosting and protective cover, parts of the plant, especially the rootstock and the young shoots, provide various edible substances.

Another fairly tall emergent plant is the arrowhead, whose generic name comes from the arrow-shaped leaves of some species. Other species have no such leaves but are still called arrowheads. The largest species has lance-shaped leaves with a very tall flowering stalk. The white flowers usually occur in whorls of 3 around the stalk, but there may be up to 12 flowers in a whorl. Beautiful pearl colored eggs of the apple snail (*Pomacea*) often attach to the stalk. Although the apple snail may be eaten by many animals, it is an important food for the limpkin and the only food for the Everglade kite.

Other emergent plants include: spatterdock, or yellow water lily, whose yellow flowers are shaped like spheres with a small opening at the top; pickerelweed, with clusters of erect leaves and spikes of violet blue flowers that resemble those of the water hyacinth; white water lily, which often grows with spatterdock, with its large circular leaves split at the point of attachment to the stalks; and water pennywort, a small plant found rooted in mud along pond margins, whose round leaves are each supported by a stem attached at its center.

The submerged plants are those that live beneath the water. Many of these plants develop dense stands that often interfere with navigation, fishing, and drainage. Common bladderwort has fine-forked, limp leaves mixed with small roundish bladders on flexible stems. Its yellow or yellowish white flowers, on long stalks, appear above the surface of the water. The bladders have a trigger system of fibers. Small aquatic animals are caught in the bladders and are digested there. Florida *Elodea* or *Hydrilla* has long, branching stems and sharply toothed leaf margins. The stems may break loose and form floating mats. It is a highly prolific plant and is replacing the larger Brazilian *Elodea*, which has similar growth characteristics. Shipment and transportation of hydrilla is banned in Florida. Marine naiad or bushy pondweed is found in alkaline waters, commonly in brackish ponds. It has stiff leaves with conspicuous triangular teeth. All portions of the plant are eaten by coots and ducks.

If the edge of a pond is marshy, it may be marked by a display of spectacular lilies, often found in other wet places. One of these is the spider lily. Its large, white flower and its long, slender tube and delicate crownlike membrane make a flashy show. The string lily or swamp lily is another graceful plant in pond margins. Its leathery leaves grow in the form of a rosette and sometimes are four feet tall. The central stalk bears clusters of five or more fragrant white flowers, each with six separate petals and prominent stamens.

As many as 20 species of ducks migrate annually to ponds, canals, marshes, and ditches. Among the more widely distributed species are the small, blue-winged teal and the rather large pintail. Inevitably, the waterfowl population will decline with the continuous decrease in wetland habitats.

Life in a pond is dynamic, but the process of succession is slow, requiring many years for an aquatic community to advance to the stage of a dry land community. Much depends upon the size and depth of the pond and the elevations of the surrounding terrain. Equally important is the type of vegetation around the margins of the pond and the length of the growing season in the vicinity.

14. POND MARGINS

The vegetation on the perimeter of a pond is constantly on an inward move, bit by bit reducing the size of the body of water. This encircling operation is just one stage in the slow process known as succession in which one type of plant community gradually replaces another until a stable, or climax, community is reached. The time it takes for this vegetation to completely overwhelm the pond depends in part on the volume of water. It depends also on the characteristics of this vegetation and the rate of its growth.

The imperceptible march into the pond is carried on by a veritable phalanx of plants, generally in three ranks: the low grasses and sedges, the middle-size shrubs, and the largest of living things, the trees. All these plants and a variety of vines contribute their leaves, stems, twigs, and roots to a ceaseless process of decay that builds up a rich soil close to or above the surface of the water. This permits the phalanx to move forward. At the same time, other changes are occurring in the whole environment, permitting other plants to gain a foothold in the new type of habitat.

The trees that grow on the edge of a pond are obviously species that require large amounts of water. One of the more common is the coastal plain willow. It often extends right down to the very edge of the water. Its bright green leaves are from two to five inches long, less than one-half an inch wide, are finely toothed, and taper to a point. The flowers appear in slender clusters known as catkins. When the fruit pod splits open at maturity it releases numerous seeds. These are covered with silky down, enabling them to be blown great distances. This accounts for the thick, far-reaching stands that often develop in marshy areas. Another tree

Pond Margins

found along watery banks is the dahoon holly, a true Florida holly. It has shiny, dark, evergreen leaves, without the usual prominent holly spines, except for a few inconspicuous teeth toward the tip of some leaves. The small, bright red fruits that develop along the stems make a good food for birds and account for the use of the plant in Christmas decorations. Dahoon holly is now a protected plant in Florida. A relative of this plant, yaupon, grows as a shrub in sandy areas along the coastal plain. The leaves of this shrub were used by early Indians to make a black, emetic brew for ceremonial activities.

A less common tree in these low, wet areas is sweet bay, the only magnolia native to south Florida. It is generally a small, slender tree with a light brown trunk often covered with many gray lichens. The dark, evergreen, aromatic leaves show their silvery undersurface in the breeze. The flower, though not as spectacular as the famous southern magnolia, is a two-inch, fragrant, cup-shaped blossom with 9 to 12 creamy white petals. Among the larger trees found in the moist, rich lowland soils are red maple, a variety of the northern red maple, and red bay, a native of southeastern United States whose fragrant leaves are one of the "bay leaves" used as herbs.

Some plants that grow to trees in other environments are often shrubby near pond margins. One of these is wax myrtle or southern bayberry. Its leaves are lance shaped with widely spaced teeth above the middle, are spotted with orange flecks on the undersurface, and are aromatic when crushed. The fruits are clusters of miniature berries coated with a pale blue wax used to make bayberry candles. Cocoplum is another plant that may grow to a small tree but generally forms shrubby thickets in moist soils. These plants often mark the boundaries of dried up ponds. The rounded, leathery, evergreen leaves seem to stand up on both sides of the stem to face each other. The fruit, sometimes cream colored and sometimes purple, is about an inch and a half in diameter, with a white, juicy flesh, used to make jelly. The kernel of seed was a delicacy of the Seminoles. This plant seems to withstand the invasion of exotics better than many other native species.

One of the tallest of the shrubs is the primrose willow, whose relationship to the true willow is only in the somewhat similar shape of its leaf. This plant can be found in all wet places, along canal banks, ditches, swamp edges, as well as pond margins. It sometimes grows as high as 10 feet, with broad, spreading branches. It is quickly recognized by its constantly blooming, two-inch flowers that have four bright yellow petals so daintily attached they drop when touched. Another large shrub, growing at times even higher than the primrose willow, is elderberry. Twelve species of this plant grow in North America. The Florida elder has small white flowers in flat-topped clusters, and its quarter-inch black fruits are edible when completely ripe.

Another shrub that blooms all year, with profuse flowering in the summer, is buttonbush. Its white flowers are unmistakable: the round heads with long, protruding, golden tipped, silky stamens resemble pincushions. The fruits are smaller, consisting of a ball of nutlets, which accounts for the common name buttonbush. These shrubs often edge down into the low, watery margins. The shrub known as saltbush derives its common name from the salty appearance of its small white summer flowers and white fall fruits. It has a habit of dense growth. Its leaves are a light green and often develop seven sharp points.

Many weedy plants grow slightly back from the edge of the pond. One of the more common of these is the large, stout herb known as pokeberry, whose reddish stems sometimes extend for as much as 10 feet. Its leaves are enjoyed by the larvae of many insects so that the plant often has a shabby appearance. Its purplish black berries, flattened globes, are a favorite food of birds. The berry juice is sometimes used as a pigment. Old leaves, the roots, and the berries of pokeberry are poisonous.

Vines grow abundantly in this moist environment, some trailing along the ground and others climbing into the trees and shrubs. Milkweed vine or white vine, always found at the edge of the pond, has clusters of waxy, starlike flowers and grows in twisted masses. Virginia creeper uses its tendrils to cover wide areas. Its stem is dark red, its leaves spread out in fives, and its small flowers are greenish. The balsam apple or balsam pear has five-parted leaves, unattractive pale yellow flowers, and delicate tendrils. Its fruit is striking: a miniature bright orange melon that splits open when ripe to reveal several seeds covered with a brilliant red pulp.

The pond is only one type of watery environment. The major wetland of Florida is the large marshy area known as the Everglades. This is the land of alligators, high hammocks, cypress heads, bromeliads, orchids, ferns, and other plants and numerous animals that thrive in its rich, humid setting.

15. ALLIGATOR HOLES

Plant and animal communities in southern Florida can survive only if they adapt to the annual cycle of a highly productive water period followed by the dry, lean seasons of winter and early spring. During times of rising water, trees and plants flourish, animal food is plentiful, and aquatic species multiply and move freely over the vast wet areas. But when the land becomes parched and food dwindles, the struggle for survival becomes intense. Millions of animals die in this periodic catastrophe, but when the rains return there is a miraculous renewal because members of each species have managed to locate a water source during the perennial drought.

Some animals burrow into the muddy peat and marl. Others crawl through the porous limestone to reach down to the water table. Some concentrate in the limited number of ponds and sinkholes that rarely go dry. Some species cannot maintain any activity at all; these retire into estivation, a sluggish state just short of hibernation. By far the most significant factor in preserving the ecology of the Everglades is the alligator holes, for at times an alligator hole is the only source of water for miles around.

Large alligators dig ponds in low places. Many return year after year to the same holes. With feet, jaw, and tail they widen these holes, ripping plants out of the ground, slashing and uprooting the saw grass, and pushing the muck and debris out onto the banks. Rich vegetation soon grows up around these muddy banks, providing a food supply and nesting place for insects, birds, and mammals. Moving right in with the alligator is a large concentration of fishes, turtles, snakes, snails, frogs, and other freshwater animals. Raccoons, heron, deer, and otter are drawn to the water hole. Long-legged wading birds, ducks, and vultures join the other tenants.

A complex food web is in operation with everything interrelated. Small fishes eat the mosquito larvae. Larger fishes and wading birds feed on the smaller fishes. Snakes feed on the frogs and crustaceans. Hawks feed on the snakes and small animals, the latter themselves voracious predators. Small alligators eat tadpoles, crabs, and minnows and are in turn eaten by turtles, raccoons, and the large wading birds. Many of these animals, especially garfish, become food for larger alligators.

What is important, however, is not who eats whom, but who lives with whom. For when summer rains come and the water rises in the Everglades enough animals of each species will have survived so that the process of repopulation can begin all over again. The pools produced by the powerful thrashing of the alligators prevent the massive decimation that the yearly drought would otherwise produce. For this reason the alligator has been called "Florida's leading reptilean citizen." Not long ago, the persistent and uncontrolled killing of these animals for the commercial value of their hides almost annihilated the species, but now the importance of the alligator to the ecology of south Florida is recognized by protective legislation. The present relative prosperity of the alligators has, however, generated a campaign to permit a modified hunting season. An obvious danger is that any opening in the protective wall may soon lead to a renewal of the slaughter that brought this near-prehistoric animal to the edge of extinction.

During the rainy season, and before the water supply becomes concentrated in the alligator holes and the permanent ponds, a sheet of water covers the Everglades and moves at a sluggish pace toward the sea. Saw grass is the most dominant plant in the immense flatland, forming the legendary "River of Grass." The Indians called the area "Pahayokee," meaning "grassy water."

For much of the year the saw grass, which derives its name from its spiny-edged leaves, is rooted in water, but it is a hardy plant, well adapted to its environment. It produces a seed which drops from the parent into the water, where it catches in the tangled mass of undergrowth and then sprouts and takes root. Although the saw grass lies over a major portion of the Everglades, the vast expanse is dotted with small hillocks, called tree islands. These islands, some of which encompass or are near alligator holes, are named for their most dominant vegetation. The smaller, low-lying islands, which are often flooded for months, are called heads: bayheads if the dominant plants are sweet bay and red bay, willow heads where there are willows, and cypress heads where there are cypresses. In the southern part of the Everglades some of the islands are on slightly higher ground where they are free from regular flooding. These islands are called hammocks, and they support such hardwood trees as mahogany and gumbo limbo, as well as a great variety of true tropical vegetation, including many species of rare ferns, orchids, and other fascinating epiphytes (air plants).

Although crocodiles may occasionally be found in the same area with alligators, each generally keeps to its own domain. Crocodiles prefer salt or estuarine water, compared with the freshwater preference of alligators. From a physical viewpoint, crocodiles can be recognized by their olive gray color compared to the black skin of the alligator, and by their narrow tapering snout, which is easily distinguished from the

Bayhead
Cabbage Palm
Cypress Head
Willow Head
Sweet Bay
Magnolia
Dahoon Holly
Bald Cypress
Coastal-Plain Willow

Anhinga
Crocodile (for comparison)
Coots
Deer
Soft-Shell Turtle
Bass
Gar
Dragonfly
Alligator
Bream
Minnow
Saw Grass
Snapping Turtle
Common Gallinule
Purple Gallinule
Pig Frog

Alligator Holes

blunt, shovel-shaped nose of the alligator. In general, the range of the alligator is much more extensive than the crocodile, and its importance to the ryhthm of life in the Everglades is more thoroughly understood.

16. HAMMOCK

Step inside! Come out of the warm, bright sunlight and into a cool, moist, shady setting. The ground is higher than the surrounding area. The vegetation is lush, dense, and varied. Overhead the crowns of tropical broad-leaved trees make a canopy through which the sunlight barely filters. A thick, tangled mass of small, crooked trees and intertwined shrubs gives an impenetrable appearance. From above, the hanging roots of a fig tree reach down to the earth to begin the routine of strangling its host tree. Air plants, orchids, and bromeliads decorate the trunks and branches of some trees. Vines, many with thick, heavy stems coiled upward, add another aspect of a jungle. Underneath is a multitude of ferns, mosses, some shade-tolerant flowering plants, stumps, logs, and other debris. Hundreds of species of small animals live here. This beautiful spot is a hammock.

A hammock is an island of trees and related vegetation that stands out from the surrounding landscape, said to be named from the Indian word for a shady place. In south Florida even a slight variation in elevation can have a marked effect on the type of growth. There are two types of hammock: the low hammock and the high hammock. The low hammock, or oak-palm hammock, is dominated by Sabal palmettos and such temperate species as live oaks. The high or tropical hammock abounds in vegetation of West Indian origin and so is confined to the coastal and southern areas where frost damage is minimal.

Because the tropical hammocks of the coastal section occupied some of the highest land in the Atlantic coastal ridge, they were the first to fall before the powerful thrust of urbanization in the 50+ mile stretch from Fort Lauderdale through Miami to Florida City. Hundreds upon hundreds of these "climax" forests that stood undisturbed for centuries disappeared, and generally only those preserved for public use remain to be enjoyed and studied.

A climax community is the final product of the process known as succession. This process is a gradual, systematic, and predictable change in the composition of a natural community until an end point, called the climax community, is reached. A climax community remains relatively stable unless there is a major change in the environment.

The concern of conservationists is whether human interference with the natural cycle of drought and flood will upset the stability and variety of this environment.

Succession takes place everywhere. The area in which it takes place may be a few square feet or many square miles. The forces of change are both physical and biological. In each community these forces produce new environmental conditions. Under these changed conditions, new species of plants and animals thrive more than the old ones, and in the competition for living space the new species displace the old. The rebuilding process therefore involves a methodical destruction of one community by the next higher community, until the climax is reached.

The nature of the climax community depends on climactic conditions. In any given area there is but one climax. This, for example, could be a grassland, a desert, or a mountainous timberland. In the region of subtropical Florida free from fire the climax community is a high hammock. The road to the high hammock can begin almost anywhere—a limestone outcropping, a sandy beach, an abandoned pine forest, a marsh, or in fresh, salt, or brackish water. The routes may be different and somewhat complex, but in the late stages trees begin to take the primary role and the end is ultimately the same.

One of the basic characteristics of the high hammock is the diversity of its vegetation. Among the many large trees are those with such enchanting names as gumbo limbo, poisonwood, wild tamarind, mastic, and paradise tree. A combination of color and form distinguishes the gumbo limbo from other trees. The thick, reddish, smooth but peeling bark of the tree is topped by massive branches spreading out at wide angles like muscular arms. It sheds its leaves in the fall and is especially striking at that time against a background of evergreens. It is one of the largest and most common native trees of the coastal region. The tree exudes an aromatic, resinous sap, which has been used as a liniment, and made into varnish. The name "gumbo limbo" is a corruption of the Spanish name for the sap—"gumma elemba."

The poisonwood tree, sometimes confused with the nonpoisonous gumbo limbo, is a medium-sized tree with a thin, flaky, reddish or orange brown bark over an inner orange layer. On old and damaged trees the bark is blotched with sticky black spots caused by oozing gummy sap. All parts of the tree are poisonous and contact with it can produce a rash as harmful as that caused by poison ivy, to which it is related. The leaves consist of three to seven glossy leaflets on long stems, each leaflet marked by a prominent midrib. The fruit is colored orangy brown and hangs in loose clusters.

The wild tamarind is a large tree belonging to the legume or pea family, whose autumn fruit is a dark red or brown flat pod about four to five inches long. The light gray bark of its trunk and the feathery, fernlike foliage on its broad spreading branches produce a typical tropical appearance. The beautiful Florida tree snails seem to prefer the bark of this tree.

The mastic, a large majestic tree that often dominates the hammock, grows to heights of 70 feet with a straight trunk crowned with stout branches. The glossy, yellow green leaves with crinkled or wavy margins on fairly long stalks flutter in the wind. The edible fruit is like an olive, with a firm yellow skin of a pleasant, rather acid flavor.

The paradise tree is very attractive with its light brown bark and its leathery evergreen leaflets. The fruit, about three-fourths of an inch long, is red, but turns purple as it matures. The paradise tree is in the family of the *Ailanthus*, "the tree that grows in Brooklyn."

Among the smaller shrubby trees in the hammock are those of the *Eugenia* species, generally known as stoppers. The leaves of these trees are quite aromatic, but the most well defined is the acrid, skunky odor of the white stopper. Three separate derivations of the word "stopper" have been suggested. Isolating one species from another can "stop" even some experts. The edible fruit will stop a case of diarrhea. And its tendency to grow in dense clusters will stop any penetration.

Because it is very tolerant of salt and grows well in sandy soils, sea grape is most prevalent along the coastal areas where it is often cut back by the winds to a large shrub with a contorted trunk. Its distinguishing characteristics are its smooth, gray to mottled brown bark, its large, leathery, orblike, evergreen leaves with prominent red veins on both sides, and edible fruits that ripen in the fall into purple or greenish white, grapelike clusters.

Among the shrubs one of the most common is wild coffee, a member of the coffee family. Its leaves are lacquered a bright green and are very conspicuously veined. The soft, juicy flesh of its scarlet fruit encloses two seeds resembling coffee beans, but these are not used as a coffee substitute. The fruits are not edible for humans, but are popular with birds. Another shrub in the coffee family is snowberry. This grows usually as a sprawling bush. Its common name is derived from the hanging clusters of small white fruits that sparkle against the green background of the plant. Another common shrub of the understory is marlberry. Its leaves are dark green, and its purple fruits are edible but not palatable.

Not surprisingly, this abundant plant community supports a multitude of animal life. The essence of the tropics is heightened by the presence of the beautifully colored tree snail, *Liguus*. More than 50 brightly polished color variations have been found in these snails in south Florida, and in many cases unique patterns are limited to specific hammocks. The snails flourish in the moist hammock environment because of the plentiful food supply of algae and fungi on the trunks and limbs of the trees. Here they hang like sparkling, fragile gems in a combination of colors that is a beautiful evolutionary phenomenon. They are especially hardy creatures, and by sealing the openings of their shells to a smooth surface they can survive in a dormant state throughout the long, dry periods of winter. Their population has drastically declined with the destruction of the hammocks and from the hunting activities of vandalizing shell collectors. Today tree snails are protected by state conservation laws.

Many other small creatures contribute flashes of color in the dappled sunlight of the hammock. Just overhead is a large, intricately constructed web of the nephila spider, whose elongated legs are striped in yellow and black. In the more open areas, and in contiguous pine forests, the warm morning air is filled with the wings of a host of butterfly species, including the everpresent gold and black zebra. You may also find small mammals, birds, snakes, frogs, turtles, caterpillars, lizards, moths, and—of course—flies and mosquitos. Every niche has its perfect occupant, and the whole environment has the stillness and peace of an exquisite cathedral.

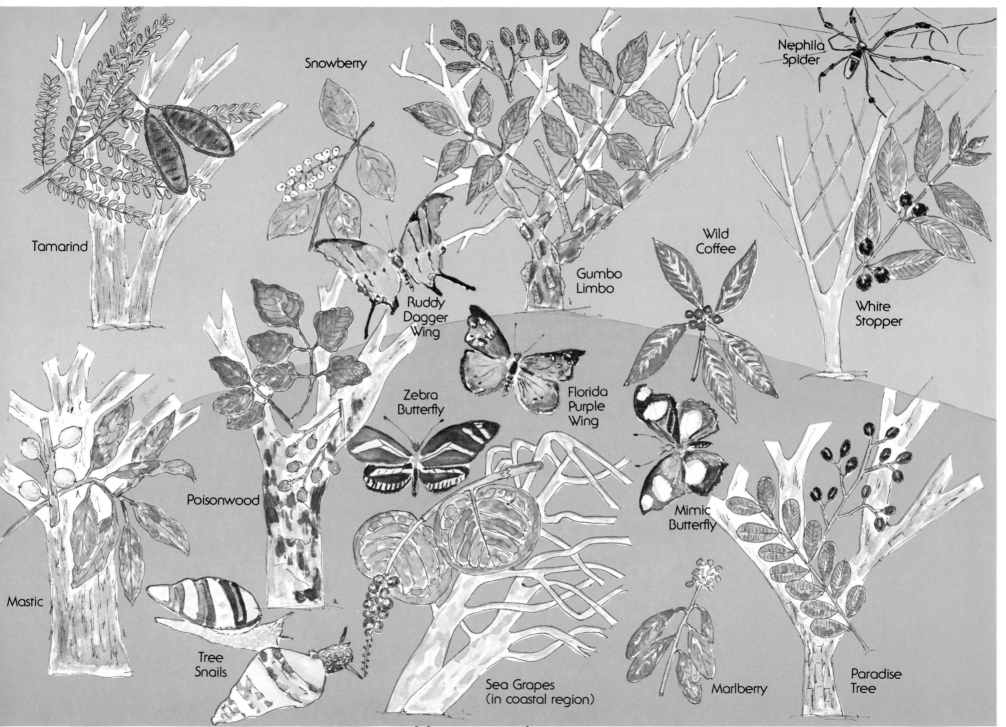

Hammock

17. CYPRESS FOREST

In the swampy, freshwater lowlands of the Atlantic coastal plain, from the Carolinas to Florida and all along the shore of the Gulf of Mexico, large watery forests of cypress trees dominate sections of the landscape. In many areas in south Florida strands or domes of these trees can be seen, but by far the largest concentration is in the Big Cypress Swamp in Collier County. At the northern tip of this region is the Corkscrew Swamp Sanctuary, preserved and managed by the National Audubon Society. This sanctuary contains the country's largest remaining stand of virgin bald cypress—the oldest trees in eastern North America. Now this natural wonder can be explored without wading waist-deep in the dark waters of the forest. A unique boardwalk, laid out through the various environmental sections, leads through an awesome interior shaded by the heavy, flat crowns on the spires of bald cypresses that reach more than 100 feet into the sky. Where there is a break in the massive canopy, sunlight shimmers on the carpets of water lettuce and duckweed that float on the quiet ponds. An elevated boardwalk has also been constructed in the small version of a cypress forest in the Loxahatchee National Wildlife Refuge, which is located in Palm Beach County.

Unlike most other conifers, the bald cypress is deciduous. It sheds its thin, flattened leaves in winter. Leafless cypresses clothed with great garlands of gray Spanish moss and displaying parched clumps of bromeliads give the bleak appearance of a ghostly, lifeless forest. The trees are bare and "bald" but not dead, for in spring bright green leaves quickly brighten the landscape. These leaves reach one-half to three-fourths of an inch in length, arranged in featherlike fashion along two sides of small branchlets. In summer loose clusters of rounded cones appear. These are about one inch in diameter and are covered with thick, irregular scales. The thin, flat seeds produced by the female cones fall when they are ripe and are sometimes caught and dispersed by the wind. The straight tall trunk of each tree with its slender outline and its branches high in the air makes a picture of impressive beauty.

A mature bald cypress tree generally has a fluted or buttressed base. It sends out far-reaching roots from which conical cypress "knees" rise out of the water. The precise function of these curious knees is not clear. Some experts believe that the knees help anchor the tree in the soft mud, while others claim they help the roots breathe underwater. When the porous bark of a cypress knee is peeled off, the hard center of solid wood can be polished to a glistening surface. Souvenir shops offer these for sale in a variety of unusual shapes.

Cypress trees growing in dry earth do not produce knees.

The trunk of the cypress is a valuable commercial product. The wood is light and easily worked and because of its habit of growth is particularly durable in contact with the soil. Because cypress is a prime lumber commodity in great demand for a multitude of outdoor uses, many of the great swamp forests have fallen first to the broadaxe and later to the chain and crosscut saws. The pond cypress is a smaller version of the bald cypress, with awl-shaped overlapping leaves that do not exceed one-half inch in length, and is usually found in the more open areas of the wetlands.

Wherever cypress trees grow, especially where they are heavily wooded, such shade-loving plants as bromeliads, orchids, and ferns are plentiful. Great variances occur in the size and pattern of the ferns. The large, prominent leather fern is a tall plant and often reaches a height of 12 feet. Masses of reddish brown sori (the clusters of cases bearing the spores) on the underside of certain specialized and erect fronds produce the "leathery" appearance. The leaves of the wild Boston fern attain heights of three feet. The sori occur in separate dots on the underside of the "eared" leaflets. The royal fern grows out of clumps of old leaf bases. The top of some of the leaves have flowerlike masses of spore cases, causing the plant to be frequently called the flowering fern. The leaves of the strap fern are long, arching blades and emerge from a short rootstock. The sori pattern, two rows in each veinal division, shows through on the face of each leaf. The marsh fern has thin, delicate leaves with sori in the lobes of the leaflets. The finely toothed edge and very thin veination identify the mid-sorus fern. Two lines of sori run along the underside of the leaflets, one on each side of the midvein.

In the more open areas of the cypress forests and in the perimeters marsh-loving trees prevail, including pond apple, guava, pop ash, dahoon holly, and swamp maple. The shrubs are represented by wax myrtle, elderberry, cocoplum, and saltbush. Vines are plentiful, especially the hemp vine, which likes to twine itself around the young cypress. Many of the trees have lichens on them.

The abundant aquatic life of the ponds provides a haven for herons, egrets, ibis, limpkins, and other subtropical birds. Woodpeckers and warblers are in abundance. The Corkscrew Sanctuary supports the largest nesting colony in this country of the rare wood ibis. Alligators and water moccasins lazily sun themselves on moss-covered logs, and the partly aquatic southern ribbon snake may not be far away. There are many water-loving plants, including arrowhead, pickerelweed, peltandra, and the long-stalked thalia, whose leaves are exceeded in size only by the palms. Overhead is the fascinating biological community of epiphytes—plants that have solved the problem of living space by growing on trees. Occasionally, a bald eagle or osprey can be spotted on the top of the tallest cypress, from which these predators can easily survey the surrounding marsh or watery expanse. The whole is a mysterious and beautiful environment that becomes tragically fragile when natural or human-made drought threatens its supply of freshwater.

18. BROMELIAD KINGDOM

Most cypress strands and some hardwood hammocks have the appearance of tropical rain forests primarily because of the clumps of plants that cling to or hang from the trunks, branches, and crotches of the trees. These air plants, or epiphytes, are defined as plants that grow upon another plant, using the latter solely for support. Although an epiphyte lives on another plant, it is not a parasite because it derives no nourishment from its host. What it needs to survive it takes from the sun, the air, the rain, and miscellaneous debris. Although the roots of these plants do absorb some water and minerals, their primary function is to anchor the plant to its situs. In the early stages of their development epiphytes took to growing in tropical trees because survival in the shaded and crowded forest floor presented insurmountable obstacles. These plants made various necessary adaptations so they could occupy the otherwise unused niches high in the trees. Further adaptations had to be made to achieve the transition from an equatorial climate with its constant supply of moisture to the Florida peninsula, where periodic droughts occur and where each winter the deciduous cypress forests give up their protective canopies.

The epiphytic adaptation is a characteristic of numerous forms of the plant kingdom. Many orchids, ferns, mosses, lichens, algae, and even trees have developed their own solution to life off the ground. A rather specialized form of epiphyte and some of the more conspicuous members of this class are the bromeliads. Because of their resemblance and relationship to edible pineapples, a number of bromeliads are often called wild pines. These are the plants that form the heavy clumps in the branches of bald and pond cypress, pond apple, and pop ash in the swampy lowlands; in the branches of buttonwood in the brackish coastal margins; and in the branches of live oaks in slightly higher areas. All these trees have a common basic characteristic essential for the survival of air plants. They have rough, deeply furrowed barks that perform two functions: they provide a surface to which the plants can anchor, and they collect and hold organic debris in their crevices.

The bromeliads are most ingenious in their adaptations. They have developed a special structural form for collecting and storing water.

Their pointed leaves are furled at the base, but then spread open to form a vaselike container for funneling rainfall and dew. This miniature reservoir becomes the center of an active environment. Mosquitos and other aquatic insects live and breed in the water, small tree frogs find shelter and moisture in the rosettes of leaves, snakes search out frogs and lizards, and birds drink from these readily accessible and almost perpetual water sources and forage for insects among the leaves. Decaying remains of insects, droppings of birds and frogs, rotting fragments of leaves and bark, and minerals in rainwater combine to form a rich food supply for the plants. This food supply is absorbed into the plant by fine hairs on the inner surface of the leaves. Additional water and minerals that drip down the tree trunks after rain showers are taken up by the bromeliads, as well as other air plants, through the appendages that fasten the plants to the host trees. Those epiphytes that do not have the architectural framework of the bromeliads must acquire their water and food suplies by other techniques.

The bromeliads have solved the problem of reproduction from their aerial habitats by combining two devices common among plants. The first is the manufacture of enormous quantities of tiny seeds, each attached to a feathery plume. Late in winter the ripe brown seed pods split open, and the air becomes filled with these windblown seeds. A heavy seed on its way to the ground would have little chance of attaching itself to the rough bark of a tree. But from the myriad of wind-driven seeds of the bromeliads some do settle in the crevices of distant trees, ready to germinate and grow if appropriate conditions develop. The second device provides for reproduction only on the site of the parent plant. With the exception of the species known as the pineapple air plant or the giant wild pine, all the bromeliads produce growing tips along their "roots." These develop into new plants to replace the dying ones. This vegetative method of reproduction accounts for the congregation of large numbers of plants and for the clumpy appearance of many of the bromeliads.

Approximately 15 species of bromeliads have adapted to the conditions in south Florida. Some of them maintain the preference of their ancestors for the moist, dark regions of the tropical forests. These grow only in the more shady areas or on the lower branches and trunks

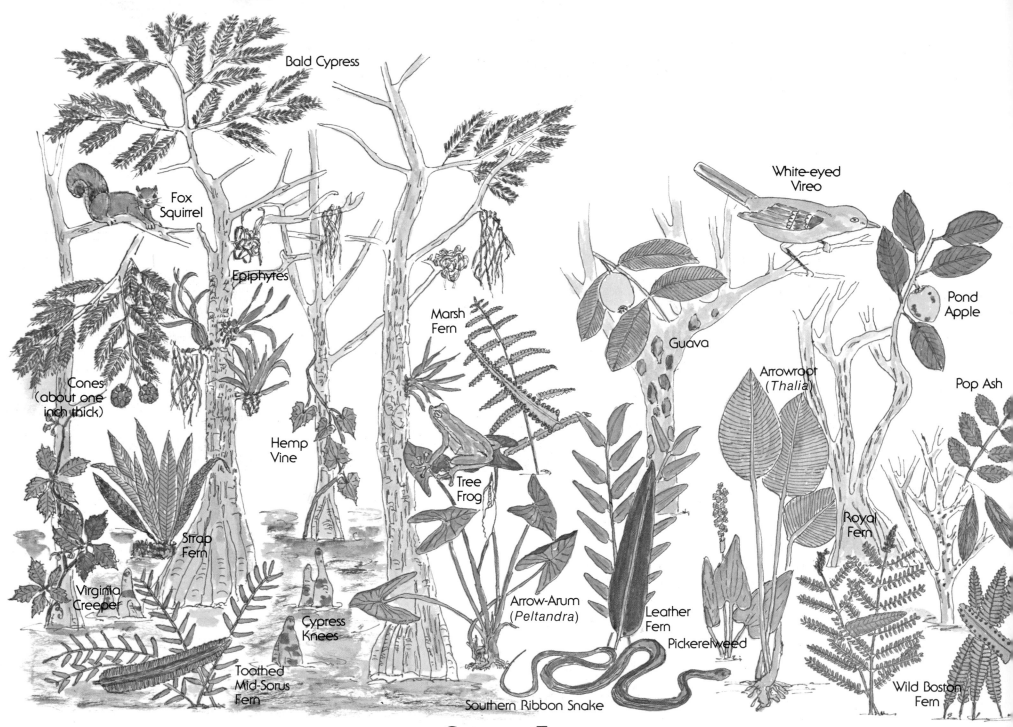

Bald Cypress

Fox Squirrel

Epiphytes

Cones (about one inch thick)

Hemp Vine

Marsh Fern

Tree Frog

Strap Fern

Virginia Creeper

Cypress Knees

Toothed Mid-Sorus Fern

Arrow-Arum (*Peltandra*)

Southern Ribbon Snake

Guava

White-eyed Vireo

Pond Apple

Arrowroot (*Thalia*)

Pop Ash

Leather Fern

Pickerelweed

Royal Fern

Wild Boston Fern

Cypress Forest

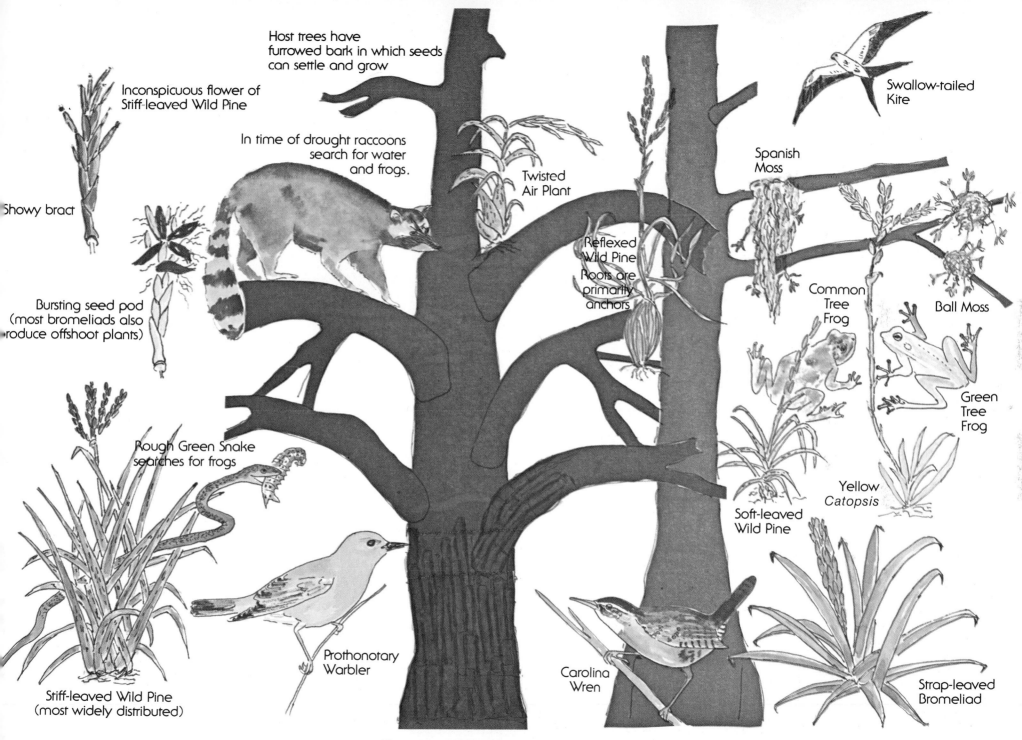

Inconspicuous flower of Stiff-leaved Wild Pine

Host trees have furrowed bark in which seeds can settle and grow

In time of drought raccoons search for water and frogs.

Twisted Air Plant

Swallow-tailed Kite

Spanish Moss

Showy bract

Reflexed Wild Pine Roots are primarily anchors

Common Tree Frog

Ball Moss

Bursting seed pod (most bromeliads also produce offshoot plants)

Green Tree Frog

Rough Green Snake searches for frogs

Yellow *Catopsis*

Soft-leaved Wild Pine

Prothonotary Warbler

Carolina Wren

Stiff-leaved Wild Pine (most widely distributed)

Strap-leaved Bromeliad

Bromeliad Kingdom

of some trees. Most of the bromeliads, however, have adjusted to sunny, open environments. This is readily apparent in the widespread strands of pond cypress where the sparse overhead foliage permits the penetration of abundant sunlight. Here particularly heavy concentrations of bromeliads can often be observed. But the increased sunlight of these exposed areas creates a greater hazard of dehydration, so these bromeliads have had to make further defensive adaptations, including thicker leaf skins, hairy surfaces, and tighter leaf overlapping. Most bromeliads bloom during the summer months. The flower spikes vary in length from two inches to seven-foot stalks. The small, almost inconspicuous, flowers are concealed in spectacular bracts. Many of these bracts are bright red and are commonly mistaken for the actual flowers.

Two species in the family of bromeliads have unique structures. Spanish moss, which elaborately drapes its supports with pendulous strands and which is considered the characteristic feature of the coastal plain, is the most widespread member of the bromeliads. The elongated stem of this plant is covered with minute gray scales that absorb the required water and nutrients and that give the plant its deathlike appearance. The swallow-tailed kite, a graceful hawklike bird, will often line its stick nest with strands of this plant. The second member of this unique pair is ball moss, which resembles Spanish moss in its general appearance, but which curls around its supporting branch or telephone wire to make the ball-like growth that gives the plant its name.

The natural enemies of bromeliads include raccoons, deer, squirrels, and rodents—all in search of food and water. Fire, hurricane, frost, and drought are perennial destroyers. The destruction of natural habitats for urbanization is an additional factor. Despite state conservation laws protecting all bromeliads, private and commercial collectors have also contributed to the decline in the population of many of these tree-clinging plants.

19. OTHER EPIPHYTES

While the bromeliads in south Florida are conspicuous and profuse members of the epiphyte "family," there are a great number of other plants that qualify as epiphytes. These also have no roots in the ground and achieve their support above the level of the earth. As in the case of the bromeliads, their principal habitats are in the cypress swamps, hammocks, and the brackish buttonwood zones, but some use other hosts for living quarters. These hosts include bushes, dead logs, and tree stumps. Florida's state tree, the Sabal palmetto or cabbage palm, is the preferred choice of certain ferns. Other air plants have chosen to establish footholds on rocks, roots, twigs, and knotholes. When living conditions on the forest floor become difficult, most anything at a higher level can develop into an acceptable perch.

The most beautiful and colorful of the epiphytes are the orchids, one of the very large families of flowering plants. There are thousands of species of this plant, and they grow nearly everywhere from the arctic to the tropics. Many orchids, particularly in the arctic and temperate zones, are terrestrial while those in the subtropical or tropical regions are mainly epiphytes. Some species grow over a wide range, but others are confined to a particular environment. No orchids are parasitic. The distinguishing feature of an orchid is its flower structure. All orchid flowers have three sepals (the outer whorl) and three petals (the inner whorl). One of the petals, called the lip, is different from the others. It is larger, more showy, and appears in a variety of exotic shapes. Projecting from the center of the flower is the fleshy structure called the column, which is a fusion of the stamens and pistils, the male and female reproductive organs.

Numerous adaptations have been made by the orchids in order to stay aloft. As with the bromeliads, they produce additional plants from buds formed on their stems. Thus, the cow horn or cigar orchid will frequently beget enormous clumps. Again, as in the case of the bromeliads, the dustlike seeds of orchid plants are distributed by the winds over very wide areas, increasing the probability of survival. Orchids have made special adaptations for conserving water. Some have reduced the number and size of their leaves, and those remaining are often tough and leathery. This reduces the loss of moisture through transpiration. A few orchids, particularly the ghost orchid, have completely eliminated their leaves and are practically all "roots." Still others, including the common butterfly orchid and the showy clamshell orchid, have smaller stems, so-called pseudobulbs, in which the plants store a supply of water. Although many orchid plants are found only in the dim cypress and hardwood hammocks, some have adapted to life in the more open and sunny areas. Once about 25 native orchids could be found in south Florida, but the same forces that have reduced the number of bromeliads have destroyed some orchid species and made others exceptionally rare.

Apart from bromeliads and orchids, other plants occur as epiphytes, such as tiny liverworts that grow on moist leaves. The family of ferns also furnishes many varieties of air plants. A good number of these ferns show a firm preference for certain supports. The large, showy serpent fern and the drooping grass fern grow almost exclusively on the trunks of the cabbage palmetto. The Boston fern also appears among the old leaf bases of the cabbage palmetto. The spike moss, the whisk ferns, and the long strap fern prefer logs and stumps. The resurrection fern is probably the most profuse of the epiphytic ferns. While it is often found in shaded hammocks, it has a strange adaptation that enables it to reach out into open, sunlit tree limbs or fallen tree trunks where its creeping rootstocks form large mats. During periods of drought it appears lifeless. The blade shrivels and curls up, showing only the dense, brown underside. When rain or heavy dew falls, the dried leaf unfolds and is transformed into a bright green plant. To solve the challenge of perpetuating the species, most ferns produce enormous quantities of minute spores that are light enough to be carried by the winds.

There are several other epiphytes of special interest. That strange partnership of fungus and algae, known as lichens, are recognized generally in greenish gray patches on tree trunks. But in a cypress forest the bright pink spots of the variety known as baton rouge can be seen on some of the trees. The herb known as oval leaf peperomia has thick, succulent stems that reach 2 feet long. It grows both in the soil and on fallen logs and trunks of living trees. It insures the distribution of its seeds by coating them with an adhesive mixture, so that the bodies of small animals become their carriers. The same is true of the mistletoe cactus, whose sticky seeds are carried on the feet and beaks of birds that feed on them. Birds and small animals also feed on and distribute the seeds of the strangler fig, but this is often the beginning of a relentlessly destructive process. The tiny seed, dropped in the branches of another tree, wins a place in the sun by developing a crown of its own above the height of the host tree. Simultaneously, it sends down long, aerial roots that hold in the ground and wrap themselves securely around the trunk of the host tree. These roots multiply and thicken and ultimately crush the host tree to death, and in its place is the strangler fig.

The warm, humid areas of southern Florida provide ideal environments for a large variety of air plants. In bloom they add exotic and dramatic decorations to the scenery of the woodlands. Their survival, against the competition of terrestrial plants, attests to the remarkable versatility and adaptability of many of nature's flora.

20. PINE FLATWOODS

Pines rank high among the more important timber plants of the world. They grow principally on dry, sandy soils of little value. Apart from lumber they yield tar, pitch, rosin, and turpentine when the trees are bled for their gum. All pines are cone-bearing evergreens with slender needles bound in bundles at the base. The needles of the slash pine, a fast-growing tree common to all parts of Florida, are from 8 to 12 inches long, dark green, shiny, and thickly set on the branches, forming a dense, symmetrical head. The needles occur in clusters of two or, very often, three in a sheath. The cones are generally 3 to 7 inches long, brown and glossy, shaped like thick carrots, with scales that are armed with fine prickles.

In northern Florida thousands of acres of woodland are devoted to the commercial production of slash pine cellulose used in the manufacture of paper and plastics. The economic necessities of this industry compel the elimination of any competing flora and fauna, with the result that these environments are neither natural nor diverse, but monotonous and endless rows of brown tree trunks.

The situation in the southern part of the state is different. One unique area, which comprises some of the highest and oldest land in south Florida, is especially fascinating to naturalists. This is the ridge extending southward on the east coast from Fort Lauderdale to Homestead and then southwest into the Everglades National Park. This rough, bare limestone ridge is often punctured by potholes and sinkholes in which the available soil has accumulated and in which tall pine trees and other vegetation are rooted. Much of the timber in these forests, a variety of slash pine known as south Florida slash, was cut to clear the way for the cities built along the lower east coast. A stand of these pines, recovering from earlier lumbering, can be seen in the Everglades National Park on Long Pine Key. Apart from this limited region of special interest, there are large, sandy sections of south Florida in which the forest cover is chiefly slash pine. These open stands, known as pine flatlands, occur in central and southern Florida on each side of the central highlands and extend southward into Broward and Collier counties.

An interesting fact about a pine forest is that it cannot be maintained without periodic fires. These fires are beneficial because

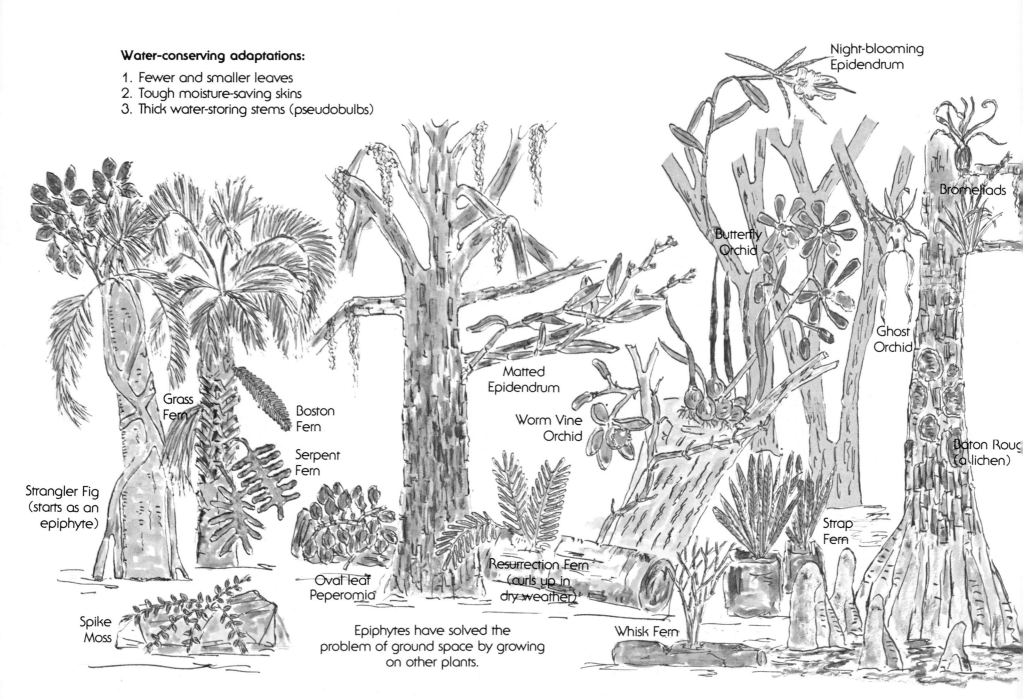

Water-conserving adaptations:

1. Fewer and smaller leaves
2. Tough moisture-saving skins
3. Thick water-storing stems (pseudobulbs)

Night-blooming
Epidendrum

Bromeliads

Butterfly
Orchid

Grass
Fern

Boston
Fern

Ghost
Orchid

Serpent
Fern

Matted
Epidendrum

Worm Vine
Orchid

Baton Roug
(a lichen)

Strangler Fig
(starts as an
epiphyte)

Strap
Fern

Oval leaf
Peperomia

Resurrection Fern
(curls up in
dry weather)

Spike
Moss

Epiphytes have solved the
problem of ground space by growing
on other plants.

Whisk Fern

Other Epiphytes

Screech Owl

Wild Grape Vine

Pine Warbler

Sneezeweed

Coreopsis

Slash Pine

Pine Needles (in clusters of two or three)

Toothed Mid-Sorus Fern

Box Turtle

Raccoon

Opossum

Pine Cone (armed with fine prickles)

Anole

Saw Palmetto

Coontie

Five-lined Lizard

Gallberry

Moon Flower Vine

Pine Flatwoods

pine seedlings require a great deal of sunlight to survive, and the periodic fires destroy those competitors that would virtually darken the environment. In a pine forest untouched by fires, small, broad-leaved hardwood trees grow in the shade of the pines. In time these shade-tolerant hardwoods overshadow the sun-loving pine seedlings, crowd them out, and eventually become the climax community as the old pines die off. What burns during a fire is the understory of the hardwood seedlings and the accumulated litter, while the pines themselves suffer little or no harm.

The high, dry lands of pine forests are susceptible to lightning fires. These natural fires may have served their function in earlier times. But, if they occur during the dry season, they can be erratic and unmanageable and may cause massive destruction. Today, periodic controlled ground fire is an accepted forest management tool, designed to eliminate the underbrush and cover before it becomes so heavy that the pines themselves face destruction from the effects of an extremely hot and unusually prolonged fire. There are also some collateral benefits from a pine forest fire: the litter is cleared away so that the pine seeds can reach the soil; nutrients bound in the surface layers of litter are released; and necessary open browsing area is created for turkey, quail, and deer.

Whenever fire is a natural factor in the evolutionary process, both plant and animal species show some kind of adjustment to it. The pine tree is fire-resistant because of its heat-resisting, corklike bark, its tall trunk, and its high branches. In addition, its growing points are protected by a tight rosette of long, green terminal needles. Those pines deeply rooted in potholes have the added protection of a fairly permanent water supply.

The most prominent plant in the pine forest is generally the saw palmetto with its distinctive palmate or fan-shaped leaf. Although at first glance it looks like a bush, it is really a tree with its trunk creeping along the ground under its leaves. Its deep roots and thick stem protect it from permanent harm, and new green shoots of leaves quickly replace those blackened by fire. Another plant in the pineland, which resembles a fern, is the coontie. These plants can survive surface burning because much of their substance is stored in large bulbous roots, the starch of which was used by the Seminole Indians and early settlers for making flour. Interspersed among the pines are occasional stands of cabbage palms whose fibrous trunks give them protection. The stems and leaves of the smaller, more delicate plants do not survive fire, but many of them, such as the moonvine or moonflower, morning glory, gallberry, wax myrtle, wild grape vine, and the ferns, regenerate quickly either from roots, seeds, or spores.

The pineland has its own society of animals. Many of them, like the raccoon and the opossum, do well in a variety of other environments. Some, however, such as the box turtle, the anole, and the five-lined lizard are especially adapted to the relatively dry, sunlit habitat. During periods of fire, insects, small mammals, and snakes move in advance of the danger zone. Bobwhites move into the freshly burned area to feed on pine seeds released from cones by the heat of a fire. A common bird among the mature pines is the pine warbler, recognizable by its yellow underparts, large white wing bars, white belly, and white tail spots. The open type of environment attracts many other birds, including woodpeckers, hawks, warblers, and owls. Among the many sun-loving wild flowers are the tickseed (Coreopsis), a common perennial that blooms throughout the year, and sneezeweed (Helenium), a springtime bloomer. Many other plants and animals contribute to the pineland ecosystem, which in its natural state can survive only with seasonal burning and freedom from such tenacious exotic species as the cajeput, the Brazilian pepper, and the Australian pine.

21. SCRUB PINE

The scrub pine forest, like the tropical hammock, is another casualty of urbanization. The high, sandy ridges formerly occupied by these forests made desirable homesites for the real estate developers of southern Florida. Only isolated fragments of this unique plant and animal community have survived, and the best examples are those preserved in Jonathan Dickinson Park, immediately north of Palm Beach County, and in the Ocala National Forest. The topsoil in these communities is a fine white sand, the remains of ancient beach dunes that contain little mineral or organic materials. The weather is usually hot and dry. It all makes for an extremely poor environment—one in which only a few species of plants have been able to survive. Those that have would surely languish in a more nutritious setting.

The basic features of this plant community are a pine forest, an undergrowth of oak and saw palmetto, clusters of shrubs, and isolated wild flowers. The sand pine in this scrub area *(Pinus clausa)* differs from the slash pine in the flatwoods *(Pinus elliottii)*; the sand pine is smaller than the slash pine, is many branched, and has a flat-topped crown. Its needles are two in a sheath, two to three inches long. The small cones persist on the tree for a long time. Some of them open when mature, while others remain closed for two to four years. When the cones open, the small winged seeds are widely dispersed by winds. Some of the cones, however, remain closed and then become overgrown and embedded in the stem and branches of the tree. When a sweeping fire completely destroys a stand of trees, the seeds in these closed cones are released, and the process of germinating and growth in the burned-over area begins again. In the forest the trunks and branches of sand pines are irregular and picturesque. Because they are hardy and salt-resistant, these trees are sometimes used as soil stabilizers in seaside landscaping, where other trees refuse to thrive.

Beneath the sand pines four different species of oaks dominate the landscape. Under more fertile conditions they would develop into fully grown trees, but in the dry, sandy soil of this type of pine forest, these oak trees are stunted, giving the general appearance of large bushes. As a group they are referred to as scrub oaks, and distinguishing one species from another may be troublesome. There is little difficulty with the turkey oak. Its leaves are large, as much as five inches long, heavily veined, and divided into five or seven lobes tapering from the base. The leaves of the myrtle oak are round, with smooth margins that are rolled back to save water. Similarly rolled back are the leaves of the sand live oak, but their oblong shapes and the whitish hairy coating on the

undersurfaces are distinctive marks. The somewhat larger leaves of the chapman or scrub oak have undulating margins that make three indistinct lobes.

In the more open areas of the forest there are dense growths of saw palmetto, whose leafstalks are covered with small bumps that swell to rigid, curved teeth near the base. This is the same palm found in abundance in the pine flatwoods. Here, too, most of the plants have sprawling trunks, with an occasional branch canting upward more than 10 feet. Another common plant that tends to grow in the open spots and that is especially indicative of this environment is rosemary. This shrub, not to be confused with the spice used in cooking, can be identified by its narrow leaves that are so fully rolled back they resemble pine needles. Another small, bushy shrub whose leaves are also shaped like needles is pennyroyal. This plant is a member of the mint family, which accounts for the minty odor of its foliage. Its flowers are light purple and grow in dense, cylindrical spikes. Other low-growing plants include the shrub pawpaw or dog apple, a member of the custard apple family with whitish, six-petalled, nodding flowers and an oblong-shaped, yellowish green fruit; and gopher apple, the ground-hugging dwarf shrub whose small white fruit is a favorite of the gopher tortoise and other small animals.

Several larger shrubs are associated with this community. Tallow-wood or Spanish plum is a scrambling shrub, armed with very sharp spines, that grows to eight feet. It has a small, yellowish flower with four petals. Staggerbush or rusty lyonia is a tall, erect shrub with clusters of small white flowers that resemble bells and that appear abundantly in the spring. Its leaves are elliptic in shape and have rolled back margins, and all but the old leaves have a distinct rusty undersurface. Shiny lyonia frequently grows in the same areas, but its leaves are flat and do not have the rusty undersurface and its flowers are pink and urn shaped.

There are a number of showy wild flowers. The golden aster is about three feet tall, with long narrow leaves, and bright yellow flowers nearly one inch across. Several species of rattlebox, members of the pea family, can be found. All have yellow, pealike flowers, and all produce pods, over an inch long, that become dark brown when ripe and rattle when shaken. Rush pink is a pink, daisylike flower whose scientific name describes its lack of leaves. One of the most spectacular of the wild flowers is blazing star. It blooms in late summer and fall with long round spikes of compact purple flowers.

Much of the white sand is free of any vegetation. There is, of course, a layer of dead leaves, pine needles, and pine cones under many of the trees. But large patches of the dry forest floor are covered with several

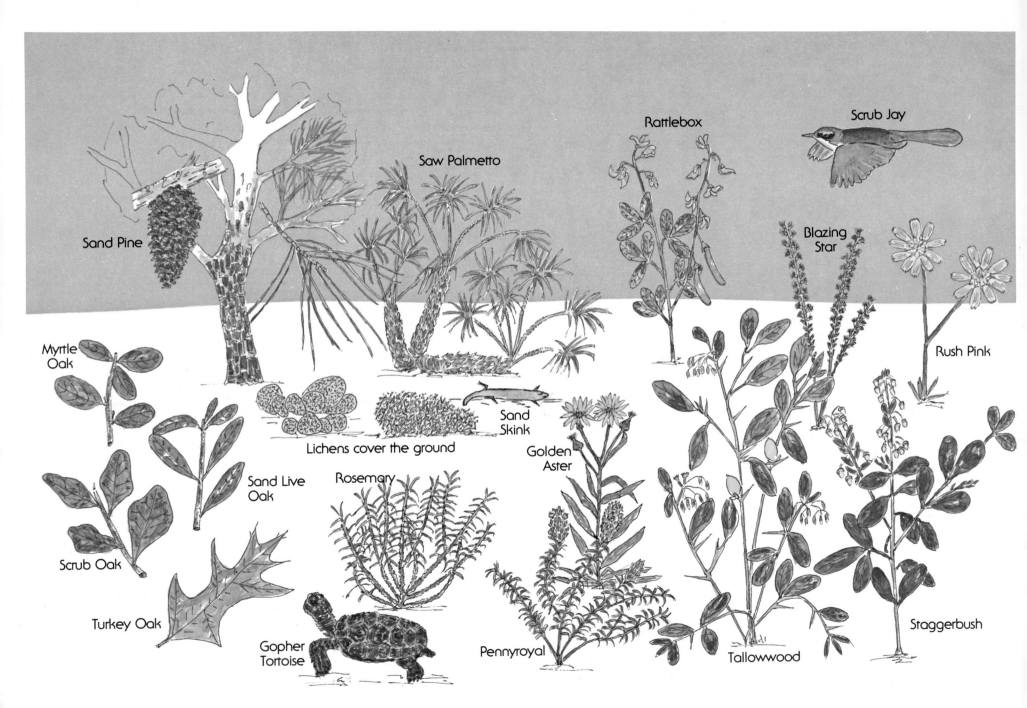

Sand Pine

Saw Palmetto

Rattlebox

Scrub Jay

Blazing Star

Rush Pink

Myrtle Oak

Sand Skink

Lichens cover the ground

Golden Aster

Sand Live Oak

Rosemary

Scrub Oak

Turkey Oak

Gopher Tortoise

Pennyroyal

Tallowwood

Staggerbush

Scrub Pine

Red-shouldered Hawk

Turkey Vulture

Red-tailed Hawk

Caracara

Sandhill Cranes

Everglade Kite (hunting for apple snails)

Bobwhites

Burrowing Owls

Prairies and Pastures

species of lichens called reindeer moss. These silvery-white non-flowering plants take on a green tint when wet. They appear in a variety of forms from a jumble of delicately intertwined miniature branches to bunches of irregularly shaped small puff balls. In these sandy patches it is not uncommon to see the small, two-inch lizard, known as the sand skink, scuttling along on his tiny legs. This is a species indigenous to this environment. Up in the trees is another lichen, named old man's beard, that has the formation of a tiny shrub, and is often mistaken for Spanish moss.

There are a number of other animals native to the scrub forest, but the most interesting and well known of these is the scrub jay. It is distinguished from the more common blue jay by its lack of a crest, its blue rather than black collar, and the brownish patch on its back. It is a timid bird and will quickly disappear into the underbrush. It makes good use of the acorns as food, as do many of the other animals in the forest. Scrub jays are among those birds that have developed the social habit of cooperative breeding. In many cases the parent birds are assisted by their prior-season offspring, so-called "helpers," in such essential activities as defending the nesting site, repelling predators, and feeding the young. Apparently the birds are so attached to the scrub environment that they have never been recorded in the eastern United States outside of Florida, although the species is represented widely in the western states.

The scrub pine forest is a good example of the adaptations made by plants and animals to fit specific environmental conditions. The scarcity of nutritional material accounts for the unique characteristics of the community.

22. PRAIRIES AND PASTURES

The land on both sides of the Kissimmee River, and extending west and southwest of Lake Okeechobee, is flat, low, and poorly drained. These vast open areas are covered with low vegetation, broken occasionally by clumps of saw palmetto and islands of cabbage palm. This is the marsh-prairie region, shaped by seasonal flooding, seasonal drought, and fire.

Florida is a land of abundant water. The primary source of this water is an annual rainfall of more than 50 inches, most of which falls during the summer months. During this season a great deal of this water filters underground to the thick, water-bearing layers of porous limestone known as aquifers. Some of the rain evaporates or transpires through plants. A good part of it, however, flows over the poorly drained land, making shallow ponds and marshy areas. During the winter months, some of these areas become dry prairies as their bottoms become exposed by seepage and baking sunlight. Thus, the marshes of the rainy period become the prairies of the dry season. Fire apparently contributes to the perpetuation of these prairies by keeping down the trees and shrubs, except where special conditions permit the growth of cabbage palm and an occasional live oak.

Long before Florida was annexed to the United States, the drier portions of this land were regarded as cow country. The Indians were capable herdsmen, and the Seminole nation maintained extensive herds. With annexation and statehood, there was a rapid influx of white cattlemen. Prior to 1900, however, these vast prairies were largely open ranges where herds of cattle roamed unchecked and where "rustling" and range wars matched those of the Wild West. The enactment of strong anti-fence-cutting laws at the turn of this century marked the beginning of large enclosed pastures and of the current methods of fine breeding, cultivated grasses, and artificial drainage. Today, beef is a major Florida product, and cattle by the thousands stand around shallow ponds, surrounded by a variety of wading birds, and graze in these open areas followed closely by the omnipresent cattle egret.

Despite these man-made changes, the prairie country still retains more of its original features than some of the other sections of Florida terrain in which so-called development has intervened. The three most characteristic birds of this community—the sandhill crane, the caracara, and the burrowing owl—are still resident species. All are long-legged for their size and can stalk the open ground with relative ease.

The tallest and most majestic of the prairie birds, often seen in large flocks, are the sandhill cranes. About the size of the great blue heron, the stately presence of these cranes, their bare reddish crowns, their soft gray coloration, and their ostrichlike tail plumes are unmistakable in the grassy landscape. Their loud, rattling calls are heard chiefly during the breeding season. They apparently mate for life, and at the time of mating indulge in a spectacular dance. Facing each other they leap into the air with outstretched wings and with feet thrust forward. Then they bow to one another and repeat the leaps, uttering their rattling calls. The nest is constructed of bunched vegetation, and the site chosen is almost always a shallow pond. Their food consists mostly of vegetables, but along with the caracara they are instinctively attracted to newly burned ground, where they eat cooked grasshoppers, beetles, and other small animals. In flight the cranes can be easily distinguished from the herons. Herons fly with their long necks folded back between their shoulders, while the equally long necks of the cranes are outstretched before them.

Another long-legged resident of the prairie regions is the caracara. This dark brown bird with black cap, white throat, and red face is essentially a scavenger. It feeds on the ground in the open country and often joins vultures at fresh kills or carrion. When approached it will often just hop away for a short distance. In addition to carrion, its diet includes snakes, mice, turtles, and insects. It generally nests in the top of a cabbage palmetto.

The third fairly common resident of the open prairies is the comical little pigeon-sized, burrowing owl. Living generally in small colonies, it has yellow eyes, its face is framed in white, it has a black collar, and its legs are rather long for its size. Its burrow is dug in sandy soil, usually not far from grassy turf and a pond. The nest is constructed of grasses, roots, and cow dung in the lowest end of the tunnel. The sand scratched out of the tunnel makes a visible mound at the entrance. The owl often perches on this mound as a lookout, and when approached will bob up and down amiably, but will finally dive into the burrow for safety. This is a fairly active bird during the daytime, and because it has begun inhabiting airports and golf courses as well as prairies, it is often an amusing sight for tourists.

One of the most handsome, and among the rarest birds of prey, is the Everglade kite. The habitat of this hawklike bird is the wet prairies, with broad expanses of low vegetation and scattered clumps of shrubs and palmettos. The kite glides and hovers over the marshes searching for apple snails (Pomacea), practically its only food item. When the kite spots a snail, the kite will slip down feet first into the water, seize the snail in claws specially adapted for grasping a slippery shell, find a nearby perch, spike the snail when it begins to emerge, and finally extract the animal with its long, hooked bill. These snails feed on aquatic vegetation; much has been written about the extensive destruction of these habitats as a result of drainage and the consequent reduction in the snail and kite population. Today, the Everglade kite is classified as an endangered species, and it can be found in its natural, undisturbed habitat only in the marshy area southwest of Lake Okeechobee. Several

water conservation areas, as in the Loxahatchee National Wildlife Refuge, are being managed in an effort to save the kite from extinction. The kites are about the size of crows and are generally recognized in flight by their dark color, broad wings, and the dark wide band on their white tails.

Two hawks are frequent inhabitants of the prairies and pastures. The red-shouldered hawk, found throughout the state and one of the more common species, nests in cypress and pine trees and occasionally in cabbage palms, but forages over grasslands and cultivated fields. The adult bird has reddish shoulder patches, but in the air it can be spotted by its rusty colored underparts and the narrow white bands on its dark tail. It feeds mainly on rodents, insects, and small birds and mammals. The red-tailed hawk, like the red-shouldered, soars over open country in search of its prey. Its nest is also often placed in the pines, or in the cabbage palms or small oak hammocks that are scattered over the prairies. It is often seen perched in a tree at the edge of the open country. It is a stocky bird, with broad wings, whitish breast, and reddish tail. All hawks are protected by Florida law.

Where the prairies merge into the open pineland, other species of birds are to be seen, including the Florida wild turkey, the ground dove, and the bobwhite quail. The bobwhite is a small, chunky, reddish-brown quail, with white throat and eyebrows in the male and buff colored in the female. The bobwhite is often seen in pastures and farmlands in coveys of about two dozen birds. It has all the qualities of a popular gamebird: it is abundant and easily available, its speed in flight is challenging to the hunter, it has the ability to provide a long hunting season, and when cooked it provides food of excellent quality and flavor.

Vegetation in the prairies varies depending on how wet the terrain is. The areas that tend to hold water most of the year have the floating, emergent, and submerged plants of freshwater ponds. On sites that drain more quickly, grasses and sedges dominate. In the spring, fresh and fragile flowers sparkle in the sunlight. There is a magical calmness about these broad, flat grasslands that reach far off into the distance. Scavengers glide gracefully in and out of fleecy clouds. Migrating birds come down to feed in the shallow ponds. The pastures are peaceful with slow-moving herds of cattle. Gentle breezes rustle through the clumps of saw palmetto. Man-made changes seem to have altered the landscape only slightly. It all seems untouched—a quiet association of exceptional plant and animal life in timeless harmony.

Enlarged branch
(leaves are small scales)

Brazilian
Pepper
(birds love the
red berries)

Cajeput Tree
(the Paperbark
Tree)

Cattle
Egret

Red-whiskered
Bulbul

Cuban
Tree Frog

Australian Pine
(not a real pine)

Armadillo

Water Hyacinth

Eurasian
Water Milfoil

Walking
Catfish

Florida
Elodea

Exotics

23. EXOTICS

In terms of ecology, an exotic is a foreign plant or animal imported and introduced into a new environment. Most developed biotic communities are made up of plant and animal species that have survived centuries of competition to establish an environment best adapted to the regional soil conditions and climate. Such communities are generally inhospitable to invaders, though as part of the natural course of change, a new species will from time to time find an ecological niche and prosper even in a mature and stable community. But this introduction is a slow process in which the invader is subjected to relentless rivalry from the older inhabitants of the ecological zone.

It is obvious, therefore, that an exotic will have a greater survival ratio if it is introduced into a disturbed area—one in which the vegetation, animal life, or land formations have been removed, destroyed, or modified. The success of exotics in Florida is due in part to the frequency and variety of such changes. Some changes are the result of natural causes: hurricanes, fires, tidal flooding, and beach erosion. Man's activities are equally as significant: drainage, spoil banks, land clearing, dredge and fill operations, and lumbering. One other factor may make Florida more vulnerable to invaders. Geographically, Florida has many of the characteristics of an island community. Compared to areas with direct land connections, island communities generally have a less diverse flora and fauna. Such an environment cannot resist invaders as well as ecosystems that have a more complete array of plant and animal life.

These various factors, plus its tropical climate, have fashioned Florida into a generous and benign host for a wide assortment of invaders. Many are harmless. Some are even beneficial and essential, particularly when they are kept under control. But of those introduced as a result of human negligence, ignorance, or indifference, some go rampant. With no natural enemies to suppress their proliferation and no harmless chemicals to control them, these newcomers upset the balance of nature, crowding out and endangering the native species, altering the landscape, and ultimately becoming uncontrollable pests.

The number of alien plants and animals that have infiltrated Florida is surprisingly large, about 50 animals and many more plants. They have come into the state in the hands or baggage of returning residents, in the holds of freighters, and in shipments to nurserymen, aquarium owners, and pet shops. There are no ready solutions to the problems posed by these invaders. In time nature may supply some restraint by way of predators or disease. At the moment, however, their populations are on the increase.

Perhaps the most visible change produced by the invaders is the alteration of the Florida landscape by three exotic trees: cajeput or the paperbark tree *(Melaleuca)*, Australian pine or beefwood *(Casuarina)*, and Brazilian pepper or, erroneously, Florida holly *(Schinus)*. The cajeput, a native of Australia and Southeast Asia, has a creamy white bark that curls off in layers. Because of its ability to transfer groundwater into the atmosphere, it was originally imported by farmers to help drain proposed agricultural areas, crowding out cypress, pine, and other vegetation. It has no apparent value to wildlife and prodigiously produces pollen that causes respiratory irritation. The Australian pine was originally introduced as a windbreak. Although its foliage resembles a pine, it is not a conifer. What appear to be needles are fine, jointed branches. It, too, has escaped from cultivation, and one of its salt-tolerant and prolific species has seized extensive strips of the coastal fringe, closing the upper beach areas to other plants. The third member of this aggressive triumvirate, Brazilian pepper, was introduced as a cultivated ornamental because of its shiny leaves and hollylike berries. Birds feed on these red berries and spread the seeds everywhere. The heavy shade of the tangled jungles produced by this tree crowd out native vegetation. The tree is related to poison ivy and produces a similar rash in sensitive individuals. In bloom it is also a respiratory irritant.

Florida is no less vulnerable to invasion by exotic animals. The nine-banded armadillo, a native of the Southwest and of Central America, has prospered so well after its introduction into Florida that most tourists know the animal only by the dead specimens seen on highways. In farmlands its rooting habit may endanger crops; in forest areas it digs into the leaf mold in search of small animals. The Cuban tree frog has travelled up the coast from Key West, and because of its larger size may capture the niche now occupied by the native variety that consumes insects harmful to citrus trees. The giant Latin American toad is already a household pest in southern Florida. The red-whiskered bulbul, a colorful singer, and the parakeet are fruit-loving birds. In large numbers they can become an agricultural threat. Since their release in Florida they have multiplied rapidly and nothing stands in the way of their abundant expansion. The walking catfish may already be out of hand. A native of southwest Asia, it has an adaptation for breathing air so that it can travel over land in wet weather. It now occupies large areas of the state, and apart from being another traffic hazard it, along with other exotics, poses a real threat to bass, bluegill sunfish, and other native

Purple Martin

Tree Swallow

Barn Swallow

Fish Crow

Red-winged Blackbird

Smooth-billed Ani

Boat-tailed Grackle

Zebra Butterfly

Meadowlark

Painted Buntings:

Male

Chipping Sparrow

Coreopsis

Female

Periwinkle

Towhee

Wild Poinsettia

Cardinal

Mourning Dove

Lubber Grasshopper

Anole

Backyard Birds

Turkey
Vulture

Black
Vulture

Strangler Fig

Sparrow
Hawk

Sea Hibiscus
(Mahoe)

Live Oak

Spanish Moss

Love Vine

Pricklepoppy

Rosary
Pea

Thistle

Life Plant

Broom Sedge

Goldenrod

Pokeberry

Castor Bean

Poison Ivy

Roadsides

freshwater game fish. Other encroachments in which humans have played a part include the fast-breeding fish known as black acaras, the myna bird, the nutria, and the starling.

The cattle egret made a natural introduction. Storm winds brought it from Africa to Florida, with a stopover in Guiana. Its success on this continent has been spectacular; in a relatively short time it has become entrenched in many parts of the United States and as far north as Canada. The cattle egret is a land rather than a water bird. It resembles the slightly larger snowy egret, except that it has a yellow bill and legs, whereas the snowy has a black bill, black legs, and yellow feet. The cattle egret is a common sight in pastureland, where it follows cattle herds for the insects attracted to their droppings or stirred up by their movements.

Other exotics have plagued Florida's waterways. The floating water hyacinth, a native of South America, was introduced by people unaware of the problems that lurked in its beautiful, orchidlike blossoms. By extravagant multiplication, through which it can double its mass in two weeks, it has covered and choked canals, ditches, streams, and lakes. The entangling leaves and strands have made many of these bodies of water useless for commercial or recreational activities. The dense growth shuts out all sunlight from the water, creating a biological wasteland under its leaves. Two submerged plants have also become pernicious nuisances: Florida *Elodea* or *Hydrilla*, with its sharply toothed leaf margins, is one of the fastest growing submerged aquatic plants in the world; and Eurasian water milfoil, with leaves in whorls with finely dissected segments, which grows equally well in fresh and in brackish water. All three plants are vigorous pests and the masses of decaying matter they produce contribute to an unnatural pollution of the waterways. Safe and economic methods for controlling these and other exotics are not in sight. Further infestation can be prevented only by some controls that will halt the casual introduction of potentially harmful species.

24. BACKYARD BIRDS

Backyards, whether on city lots or suburban acres, can afford good opportunities for bird watching—not so much for any scientific pursuit, but for the sense of wonder and delight in observing birds in all their wild and magical freedom. South Florida has always been known for its large concentrations of permanent and seasonal bird populations. They can be seen in the city and suburbs, as well as in the forests, meadows, marshes, swamps, mud flats, and seashores. The number of birds attracted to any particular backyard will depend largely on the availability, constancy, and variety of their basic needs for survival—food, shelter, nesting sites, and water.

Many species of birds can be seen in the course of a year. Thousands pass through as migrants. Others come from the tropics to nest. Some that nest in the north winter here. Then there are permanent residents that remain year-round. Although different species prefer different habitats, a properly managed backyard can be made attractive to a variety of birds by the right mixture of trees, shrubs, vines, and other plants.

Trees are essential. A single tree, like a live oak, is a miniature world of its own, supporting an abundance of life and serving a number of purposes. The crown gives shelter; the rough bark provides food in the form of grubs, beetles, and other insects; the branches and Spanish moss become nest-building materials; and the acorns are eaten by birds and other animals. There are other trees, shrubs, and plants that are particularly attractive to birds, for their shelter and for their seeds, nuts, berries, nectar, and fruits. These include elderberry, beautyberry, pokeberry, honeysuckles, trumpet vine, orange jasmine, hibiscus, and sunflowers.

Generally a backyard is a difficult place in which to produce natural food either in sufficient or constant quantities. Supplemental feeding for seedeaters can be corn, peanuts, millet, sunflower seeds, or commercial mixtures. Fruit eaters enjoy raisins and chopped apples. Suet in a wire or plastic holder is a high-energy food, important in colder weather, and stale bread crumbs are perennial favorites. Drinking and bathing water is especially important and will add a number of species to the backyard inhabitants. A small pool with dripping water is ideal, but a wide, shallow birdbath, regularly cleaned and constantly filled with fresh water, will suffice. It is at the pool or birdbath where birds become subject to the closest observation.

Some features of bird life have a direct bearing on the environment in which they live. Their food habits are especially important to man. The diets of many birds include a variety of animal foods. The insects, rodents, and other pests they eat help substantially in the control of many creatures that would otherwise plague humankind. During the period when birds are feeding their young, some insect eaters bring food to the nest every two or three minutes. Even seedeaters and fruit eaters often feed their young large quantities of insects for the protein and other nutritional substances required for their growth. At certain stages young birds must consume their own weight in food each day in order to develop normally. The number of pests destroyed by the estimated world population of one hundred million birds is incalculable.

Birds have been able to survive in all parts of the world and in all conceivable environments because of their remarkable adaptive proficiencies. Each species is disciplined in a pattern of survival which, in the course of the evolutionary process, has achieved a level of accomplishment best suited for the particular environment to which that species is limited. It is estimated that there are in the world some 9,000 species of birds, and that about 650 species live and breed in the area of North America north of Mexico. An abridged checklist of birds to be seen in Florida prepared by the Florida Audubon Society lists 300 species.

In the evolutionary process that produced this substantial diversification, the backyard birds represent the most recently evolved species. This is the order of birds known as the passerines. It includes more than 5,000 species and all the families of songbirds. They are all relatively small land birds with four toes, all on the same level. The hind toe is as long as the middle front toe—an effective adaptation for grasping a perch. They are generally known as perching birds, and as wire sitters in the urban areas. Except for the pair of painted buntings, the illustrated perching birds are the male of the species. The markings of the female are often very different.

The sight of a pair of painted buntings is enough to excite and fascinate the most lethargic observer. The red cardinal is unmistakable with its prominent crest and large beak; no other bird is like it. The grackle is easily identified by its iridescent feathers and wedge-shaped tail. Smooth-billed anis live in groups and build a joint nest. They are not passerines, but they look like grackles except for their short, thick bills. The red-winged blackbird is handsomely military in red shoulder patches trimmed in yellowish tan. The mourning dove has been named for its melancholy call—"Cuoo-oooo-oooo-oo." A slender bird, it moves with dainty steps. The blue-backed barn swallow has pointed wings and a deeply forked tail. The tree swallow is an accomplished aerial acrobat. The bright rusty cap and prominent white eye stripe identify the chipping sparrow. The purple martin, the largest of the swallows, is a gregarious bird even when nesting. One of the identifying signs of the towhee is its distinctive song "Drink your tea." Many birds have not adjusted to living close to human habitation. From time to time, however, some wander into backyards. The meadowlark, with its bright yellow breast, is more often seen in the open areas perched on a fence. At times it may be seen in the suburban areas. The fish crow, somewhat smaller than the common crow, is seldom seen far from water. It can occasionally be attracted to the backyard by miscellaneous food scraps.

While most of the birds attracted to the backyard will be the more common species, many of these will be among the more interesting and picturesque. The best time to see birds is in the early morning. Bird activity lessens as the sun rises and does not resume again until late afternoon. Recognizing a bird by its name adds a special pleasure to the fascinating experience of watching the courting, nesting, feeding, singing, and fighting patterns of these remarkable animals.

25. ROADSIDES

A visitor's first contact with the landscape of south Florida is frequently made on one of its many roadsides. These are the areas in which the ground has been cleared, the topsoil stripped, and the environment otherwise disturbed. It is precisely this type of area in which exotic plants can take root and flourish, and in which they can often foreclose native species from recapturing their original habitats. Nevertheless, there are native plants that have the same pioneer characteristics, and these will also enter disturbed areas and begin the process of botanical development. Many of these plants are fast growing weeds that have efficient methods of dispersing their seeds and can thus crowd out other plants by densely covering open areas with their own foliage. In some roadside areas native trees have been left undisturbed or have been planted along with foreign trees as part of beautification projects.

The trees along the roadsides consist generally of a combination of exotic and native species. Among the exotics are the three plants that have already produced a marked change in the landscape. The cajeput or paperbark tree, the Australian pine, and the Brazilian pepper. The native trees often include the live oak, the strangler fig, and the sea hibiscus. The live oak is the most popular of the many Florida native oaks. It is a shade tree of majestic character with a short, stout trunk that divides into several large limbs with nearly horizontal branches. It has a wide-spreading crown and is never completely devoid of foliage. It's trunk and branches, covered with rough bark, are often heavily decorated with Spanish moss and a variety of other air plants. The inch-long acorns are edible when roasted and are an important food for animals and birds.

Several different species of fig trees are evident along streets and roadsides. Among the species introduced from other countries are the common fig, the fiddle-leaf fig, the benjamin fig, the Indian rubber fig, and the banyan. The two native fig trees, the strangler fig and the short-leaf fig, are generally part of the rich vegetation of the hammock areas. At times the strangler fig escapes to the roadsides and exhibits there its strange habits of growth.

If the roadside is bounded by moist soil, the mahoe or sea hibiscus will flourish. This tree, a member of the mallow family, is valued for its dense evergreen foliage and its year-round flowering. It has large round leaves, four to eight inches long, with a heart-shaped base and an abruptly pointed tip. Its showy flowers, four inches in diameter on long stalks, have five overlapping petals that are yellow when they open in the morning, changing to maroon before falling. The mahoe is a very fast-growing tree rarely reaching more that 15 feet in height, often with overhanging and extending branches that spread out around its base in a wide circle. Apart from its use in highway beautification, it is a good specimen for seaside planting because of its tolerance for salt. With the live oak and fig trees, the mahoe plays a prominent role in creating a tropical background for many of the southern roadsides.

Most other roadside plants can be divided into four groups: shrubby herbs, vines, flowers, and grasses. A most conspicuous herb is the castor bean, a native of Africa, that can grow into a shrubby thicket as high as 15 feet. The large leaves are cut into seven to nine pointed stars with prominent red ribs. The seeds, from which castor oil is extracted, are contained in spiny pods that grow in attractive clusters at the end of the branches. All parts of the plant are poisonous. Another large, stout herb, a commonplace plant along pond margins and in other moist areas, is pokeberry. A smaller plant often seen along the roadsides is the succulent perennial from tropical Africa known as life plant. Its common name comes from the fact that new shoots will sprout from the edges of a single leaf picked from the plant. The dark red flowers hang from the top of the stalks like clusters of delicate bells.

Three of the various vines that run along the roadsides are poison ivy, love vine, and rosary pea. The most versatile of these is poison ivy. It can run low over the ground, it can take on a bushy, erect character, or it can climb high over trees and walls. Contact with any part of the plant can produce severe skin eruptions and irritations. The plant is identified by its three smooth, light-green leaflets that turn red in the winter. The flowers are whitish green and the fruit a waxy white berry. The love vine starts in the ground, finds a convenient plant on which to climb, gives up its ground root, and then becomes a parasite living off the juices of its host. Its leaves are inconspicuous, but its threadlike, twisting stems grow in tangled layers that will often blanket large shrubby areas with a yellowish orange network. Another vine that has a tendency to grow on other plants is the fragile, woody plant called rosary pea or crab's-eye vine. It has a delicate leaf with 20 to 30 leaflets. But its conspicuous feature is its seedpod, which splits open when ripe to expose glossy scarlet seeds, each with a black tip. These have been used for stringing rosaries and necklaces, but the practice is hazardous for the seeds are among the most poisonous in Florida, and even a prick from the stringing needle is dangerous.

Of the many wild flowers that decorate the roadsides the goldenrod provides the most spectacular display. In late summer and fall masses of brilliant color are provided by the loose clusters of tiny, golden yellow flowers blooming at the top of slender stems. Many species flourish in south Florida; these can be distinguished from one another by the differences in stem, leaf, and flower. A very distinctive roadside flower is the common thistle. The prickly wings of its dark green leaves, the spreading spines of the flower envelope, and the dense clusters of the magenta florets are unmistakable. The flowers are very heavily scented, and bumblebees often become intoxicated with their rich honey. A less common flower, with prickly leaves similar to the thistle, is the prickle-poppy. Its leaves are very light green, and its flower petals are bright yellow. It is a cultivated plant, a native of Mexico, that has escaped to the roadsides and other waste areas.

No roadside is complete without its grasses. These are by far the most powerful protectors of the soil against the erosive forces of wind and water. Three families of plants have a "grasslike" appearance: grasses, sedges, and rushes. Because many of these plants are superficially alike and do not flower conspicuously, isolating their individual marks of recognition involves a special competence. One of the most common of these plants is the three-foot high broom sedge, whose stems display feathery tassles of seed in the fall.

Plants found on the roadsides are often seen in such other places as pastures, ditchbanks, abandoned farmlands, railway banks, and spoil beds. They are also to be found in cities and towns in open areas that have been disturbed by surrounding development, and many of the plants seen in these latter areas are similarly prevalent on the roadsides.

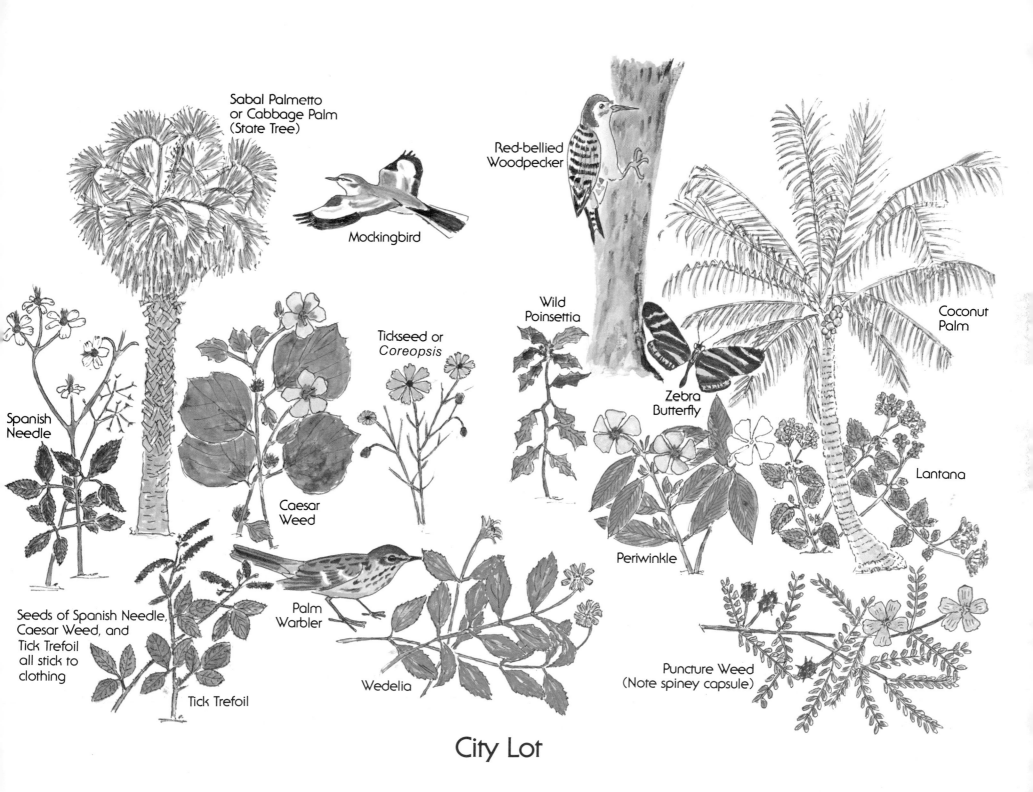

Sabal Palmetto
or Cabbage Palm
(State Tree)

Mockingbird

Red-bellied
Woodpecker

Coconut
Palm

Wild
Poinsettia

Tickseed or
Coreopsis

Spanish
Needle

Zebra
Butterfly

Caesar
Weed

Lantana

Periwinkle

Seeds of Spanish Needle,
Caesar Weed, and
Tick Trefoil
all stick to
clothing

Palm
Warbler

Puncture Weed
(Note spiney capsule)

Tick Trefoil

Wedelia

City Lot

26. CITY LOT

City lots are those plots of ground in urban neighborhoods that have been allowed to grow on their own into tangled masses of miscellaneous plants. Many of them fall into the category of disturbed areas in the sense that changes in environmental conditions have been produced by the pressures of nearby development. Pedestrian and vehicle traffic, removal of valuable plants, dumping of waste material, and other similar factors all contribute to these changes. The result in many cases is a tropical wilderness consisting of an intriguing combination of native species and exotic invaders.

The most visible plants are the palms. Florida is palm country, and wherever one goes several different kinds of palms are sure to be seen. Although there are many native and introduced varieties, most palms we see belong to about a dozen species. The palm family is divided into four groups according to their leaf characteristics. One group, the palmates or fan palms, consists of those palms whose leaf segments radiate like a fan from a common point. In the largest group, the pinnates or feather palms, numerous leaf segments give the appearance of a feather as they protrude from a central leaf stalk. Palms with some leaf segments radiating and others attached along an extended leaf stem are in the group known as costapalmates. The smallest group consists of the fishtail palms, whose leaflets have a triangular shape. Many people living in the tropical areas of the world depend upon palms for food, clothing, chemicals, waxes, lumber, and shelter.

Two of the most frequent inhabitants of city lots are native palms—the coconut palm and the cabbage palm. The coconut, one of the featherlike palms, has an unknown origin. Over the centuries, however, it has become the most numerous palm species in the world. Its curving trunk, which sometimes reaches as high as 100 feet, and its drooping leaflets together make the single most representative symbol of the picturesque tropics. But now the coconut palm, as well as the Christmas or Manila palm, are under attack by the disease known as lethal yellowing, the nature of which is still a mystery to botanists. The disease was first discovered in the Florida Keys in 1955, and it has since moved as far north as Stuart. It now threatens the destruction of millions of trees. Lacking a solution to this threat, the Malayan dwarf palm, a strain apparently resistant to lethal yellowing, is being planted throughout the state to take the place of the presently doomed coconuts.

The other prominent palm is the official state tree of Florida, the cabbage palm or Sabal palmetto. This palm, one of the costapalmates, grows profusely throughout most of the state, and because of its hardiness is unsurpassed for roadside and city planning and highway beautification. The plant is named for the large terminal bud or "cabbage" at the top of the trunk, which can be cooked and eaten as a vegetable but removed only at the risk of losing the tree itself. The trunks of these trees are used for pilings, and the leaves are used for baskets, mats, and hats. Old leaf bases persist on young trees, encasing the trunks in crisscrossed "boots," but the trunks eventually become smooth. The tree can grow to 80 feet tall.

Three of the plants found on city lots, as well as on other waste places along roadsides, are Caesar weed, tick trefoil, and Spanish needle. Each of these plants produces seeds that stick to rough surfaces of clothing and animals, assuring their wide distribution. An efficient seed-dispersal mechanism is a common characteristic of most pioneer plants—the first plants to appear in newly cleared areas. Caesar weed, a hairy-stemmed herb or shrub that can grow up to nine feet tall, has large, oval leaves and small pink flowers that bloom all year. The fruit when mature is a small brown pod covered with stiff bristles. Tick trefoil usually grows as a prostrate shrub and for that reason has been used as a substitute for grass, particularly since it is disease and insect free and can be walked upon. Its leaves are compound with three elliptic leaflets, and its fruit is a thin, flat pod of several joints with hooked hairs that cling like ticks. The last of this clinging trio is Spanish needle or beggar ticks, a member of the aster family that grows almost anywhere in sandy soil. Its showy, daisylike flower with a yellow center and five white petals can be seen all year. The fruit is a two-pronged, needle-shaped seed, accounting for both of its common names. Another prevalent plant on cleared land, and even more frequent on sandy shores, is the puncture vine or yellow burnut, a trailing herb with reddish slender stems whose seeds are carried by ocean currents to most tropical coasts. Its everblooming, primroselike, bright yellow flowers, that open in the morning and begin to close at noon, often make extensive carpets of color. This vine is used as a ground cover but not where foot traffic occurs, since its spiny seed pods are painful to bare feet and can even penetrate soft-soled footgear.

Many other flowering plants thrive in city lots and open fields. Lantana or shrub verbena, a strong-scented shrub often seen in pinelands, produces circular clusters of tiny flowers varying from whitish or yellow to pink to orange to scarlet. Its seeds are extremely poisonous. There is a purple variety often used in home landscaping that does not produce many seeds. Periwinkle, an upright plant originally from Madagascar, blooms throughout the year and grows almost everywhere. Some blossoms are pearly white, others pink or purple with deep rose centers. Dwarf varieties of periwinkle are used as ground covers. Another ground cover is wedelia, a perennial creeping herb from tropical America, with opposite, bright green, rough-textured leaves, that blooms constantly. It has a yellow, daisylike flower, each of its 8 to 12 petals tipped with 3 lobes. The wild poinsettia introduces a different color into the landscape. This plant, sometimes called fire-on-the-mountain, is a small relative of the familiar Christmas poinsettia. Its tiny flowers, clustered at the tip of the stem, are surrounded by leaves that have red or yellow blotches. One plant may have three different types of leaves: ovate, narrow, or fiddle shaped. A common plant of all open areas and one that blooms most of the year is tickseed or *Coreopsis*. It is a perennial, often growing in clumps and producing numerous of its yellow, brown-centered, daisylike flowers on tall, almost leafless stems.

No area in south Florida is free from birds and butterflies. Even the city lot has its share. The mockingbird, Florida's state bird, is everywhere. Its lively chatter, repeating phrases many times, often imitates the songs of other birds and contributes substantially to the nighttime chorus. Its two white wingbars, its long tail edged in white, and its habit of flicking its tail from side to side make for easy identification. Wherever there are trees there are red-bellied woodpeckers, a common woodpecker in south Florida. The distinguishing marks are not a red belly but a red head, and a black and white ladder-back. Its bobbing head can often be seen on the trunk of a coconut palm. The palm warbler is an abundant winter resident in south Florida. It has bright yellow undertail feathers and a yellow breast with light brown streakings. It can generally be spotted by the constant up-and-down flicking of its tail. Butterflies are also plentiful, especially the zebra with its unique shape and black and gold markings.

27. STREET AND GARDEN PLANTINGS

The streets and gardens in the cities of south Florida have become hosts to a large variety of decorative plants imported from all over the tropical world. Trees, shrubs, and flowers have been brought in to add colorful blossoms and picturesque forms to the areas that immediately surround both residents and visitors. It is sometimes surprising to note how thoroughly some of these imports have overshadowed native varieties in the man-made landscapes. The pleasure of observing these plants is plainly enhanced by an ability to identify them by name and an understanding of some of their habits of growth. Of the many different species, 24 of the more common plants are discussed here. Some knowledge about these should make living and visiting in the urban areas a more pleasurable experience.

ALLAMANDA (*Allamanda cathartica*)
This native of Brazil has a tubular, waxy, golden blossom that grows on a sprawling vine. The leaves are thick, glossy, and pointed. It is a fast grower and flowers throughout the year. There are several varieties of this plant, one of which produces a purple blossom.

ASPARAGUS FERN (*Asparagus densiflorus 'sprengeri'*)
This is a durable vine from South Africa used for moist, sunlight areas. The stiff arching stems grow to three or four feet, and the graceful branchlets give the appearance of the fronds of ferns. Small white flowers are followed by colorful red berries. It grows thickly, and because of its easy maintenance is used extensively as a ground cover.

BOUGAINVILLEA (*Bougainvillea glabra*)
Grown generally as a vine, the showy parts are the bracts that surround the small yellow flowers. The bracts come in a variety of colors—purple, orange, red, and salmon, and are so thin the plant is often called the "paper flower." The stems have very heavy thorns. With plenty of sunshine, the Brazilian plant will bloom profusely in almost any soil, giving a typical tropical effect.

CHRISTMAS OR MANILA PALM (*Veitchia merrillii*)
The common name for this Philippine Islands palm comes from the brilliant red fruit that hangs in clusters and matures in December. The tree has a light green upper column, crowned with stiffly arched leaf stems, and is often called a little royal palm. The base of the trunk is swollen. Because of its beauty, this native of the Philippines is now quite common.

CROTON (*Codiaeum variegatum*)
This shrub, native from Fiji to Australia, has been cultivated so that its leathery leaves now are grown in a variety of colors, shapes, and patterns. Numerous different species all provide a mass of form and color with a distinctive tropical effect. They are a favorite for foundation planting.

CROWN OF THORNS (*Euphorbia milii*)
This sprawling shrub plant, a native of Madagascar, looks like a cactus but is not. It has cylindrical stems that are thickly covered with spines, with small flowers that are surrounded with saucerlike bracts in varying shades of red. The plant thrives in any good sunny soil.

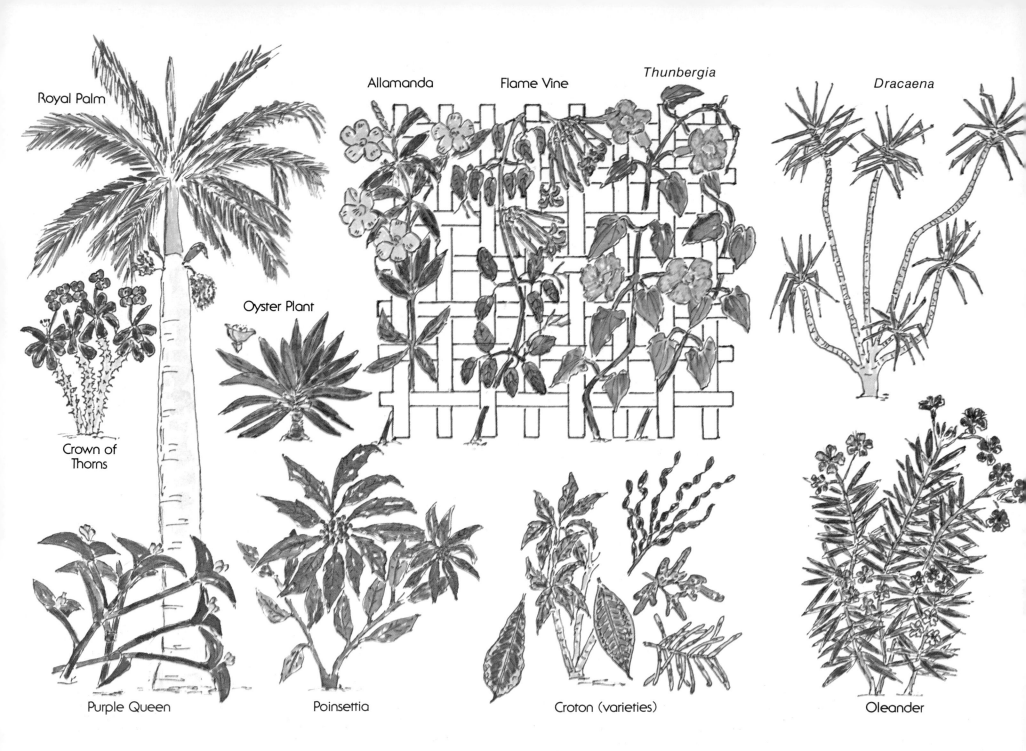

Royal Palm

Allamanda Flame Vine *Thunbergia* *Dracaena*

Oyster Plant

Crown of
Thorns

Purple Queen Poinsettia Croton (varieties) Oleander

Street and Garden Plants 1

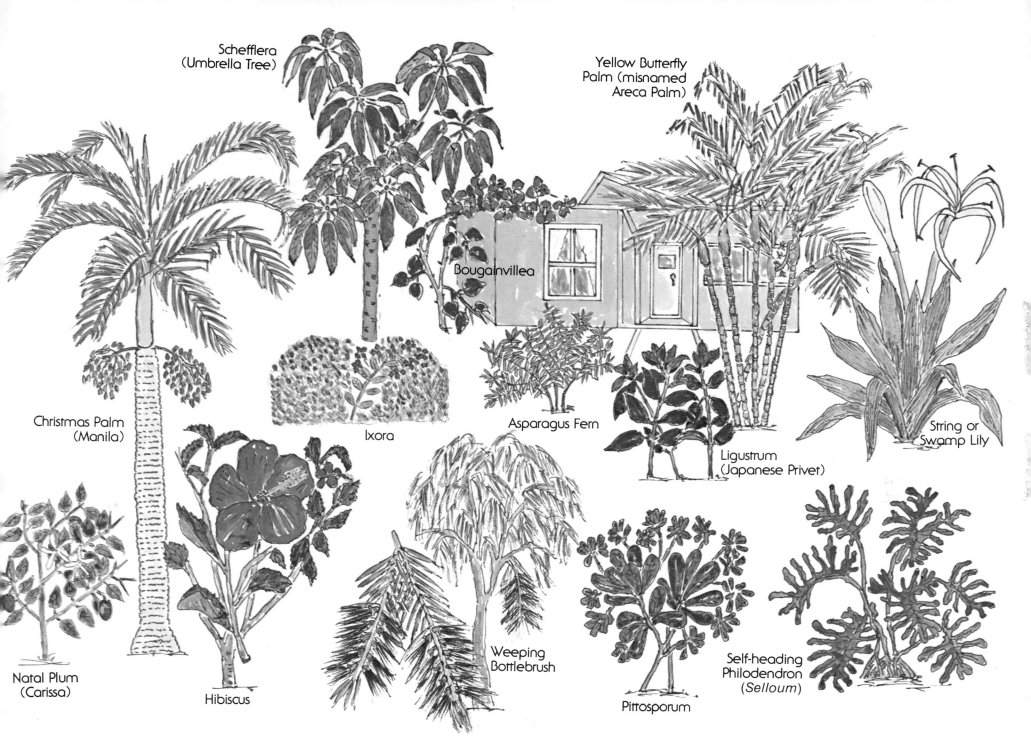

Schefflera
(Umbrella Tree)

Yellow Butterfly
Palm (misnamed
Areca Palm)

Bougainvillea

Christmas Palm
(Manila)

Ixora

Asparagus Fern

Ligustrum
(Japanese Privet)

String or
Swamp Lily

Natal Plum
(Carissa)

Hibiscus

Weeping
Bottlebrush

Pittosporum

Self-heading
Philodendron
(*Selloum*)

Street and Garden Plants II

DRACAENA (*Dracaena marginata*)·
Clumps of this graceful shrub, native to tropical Africa, sometimes called monkey palm, are often used for accents in foundation plantings or doorway groupings. It has a narrow woody stem on which a diamond pattern is left by its dead leaves. The living leaves, each soft and swordlike, form an odd-shaped tuft at the top of the stem. There are several different species, each varying in size and color. All species make good potted plants for patios and for indoor areas with modest daylight.

FLAME VINE (*Pyrostegia venusta*)
This native of Brazil owes its name to the blazing display of orange it provides during the winter months. Its flowers are slender, two-inch tubes with lobes that curl back, and its leaves are a glossy, bright green. It is fast growing and by using its tendrils can smother a full grown tree if not kept in bounds.

HIBISCUS (*Hibiscus rosa-sinensis*)
Because crossbreeding is easy, there are all sizes, shapes, and colors of hibiscus. The brilliant red variety is one of the most popular colors. It grows as a shrub, and is used as a hedge and for foundation planting. The flowers will not wilt for a full day after picking and are therefore frequently used in household displays. This native of China is one of the most spectacular tropical flowers.

IXORA OR FLAME-OF-THE-WOODS (*Ixora coccinea*)
This shrub is a native of the East Indies. The small scarlet flowers group together to cover this compact shrub with a sheet of flame. The leaves are glossy green. The plant is used as a hedge or for foundation planting. The flowers last well when cut and are used frequently in arrangements. There are other color varieties of this plant.

LIGUSTRUM (*Ligustrum japonicum*)
Native to Japan, this evergreen shrub is very similar in appearance to the northern privet. It is sometimes called Japanese privet or wax-leaf ligustrum, the latter a reference to its glossy, dark green leaves. Like pittosporum, it can withstand heavy pruning. In the springtime it has panicles of creamy white flowers.

NATAL PLUM (*Carissa macrocarpa*)
This many branched, medium-sized shrub is a native of South Africa. It has waxy, white, one-inch blossoms that look like stars, small dark green leaves, and thorny stems. Its fruit is an edible red berry used to make jams. The plant is especially recommended for hedges.

OLEANDER (*Nerium oleander*)
This large shrub from Asia Minor is not only poisonous if taken internally, but food cooked on its wood can also be poisonous. Single or double blossoms grow in clusters at the tips of the branches. It is a hardy, fast-growing plant, it blooms continuously in open sunshine, and its blossoms come in a variety of colors, from crimson to pink to white.

OYSTER PLANT OR MOSES-IN-A-BOAT
(*Rhoeo spathacea*)
The picturesque name for this tropical American perennial comes from the small white flowers in conspicuous boat-shaped bracts that bloom near the base of the leaves. The long, flat, succulent leaves, green above and purple underneath, grow in little clumps. The plant makes a good ground cover or a herbaceous border—either in sun or shade.

PITTOSPORUM (*Pittosporum tobira*)
This hardy shrub is native to China and Japan. Its dark green, leathery leaves, turned down at the margins, are borne in whorls at the end of twisted gray branches. Because it can stand severe pruning and will grow in either sun or shade, it is a favorite for foundations and hedges. It has a creamy white, mildly perfumed springtime blossom. It does best in rich, well-drained soil. It is very tolerant of salt and is generally recommended for seaside planting.

POINSETTIA (*Euphorbia pulcherrima*)
This native of Mexico and Central America, with variously lobed leaves and brilliant red bracts, is associated with Christmas festivities. Although red is the most popular, there are pink, yellow, and white varieties. The true flowers are yellow and almost inconspicuous. They bloom for long periods of time, but produce best if pruned back sharply once or twice a year, but not after Labor Day.

PURPLE QUEEN (*Setcreasea pallida*)
This native herb of Mexico is often called giant wandering Jew. It has eight-inch long, brittle, purple leaves on running, succulent stems. Its flower is delicate, three-petalled, and light purple. It grows close to the ground, in sun or shade, and is used primarily as a ground cover.

ROYAL PALM (*Roystonea elata*)
The Florida royal palm is a noble tree, often reaching 100 feet in height. The trunk is grayish white, heavy, bulging at the base and tapering to a long, bright green crownshaft. This palm is used mostly for avenue and street planting in rows on both sides of the street. Formal in appearance, it needs space and is incongruous with small home landscaping.

SCHEFFLERA (*Brassaia actinophylla*)
Sometimes called the umbrella tree, this native of Austra-lia can be a single trunked or a multiple trunked tree. Its glossy leaves are composed of five to ten oblong leaflets connected on a long stalk in the shape of an umbrella. Its summertime blossom is a spectacular whorl of small red flowers at the top of the tree. It is a good specimen tree as well as a favorite potted plant.

SELF-HEADING PHILODENDRON
(*Philodendron selloum*)
The distinguishing feature of this native of Brazil and Central America is its deeply lobed leathery leaves. This leaf shape produces a typical tropical effect in the background of gardens.

STRING OR SWAMP LILY (*Crinum americanum*)
This member of the amaryllis family is an herb that grows in a rosette form from a large, fleshy, rotund bulb. It grows wild in the swamp, marshes, and riverbanks of Florida and along the Gulf Coast. It can be planted around the edges of pools, and despite its natural watery habitat can be grown successfully in sunny soil that is only moderately moist.

THUNBERGIA (*Thunbergia grandiflora*)
This stout vine from India, sometimes known as sky vine or Bengal trumpet, produces racemes of three-inch, funnel-shaped, sky blue flowers. It grows fast almost anywhere and blooms nearly all year. The flowers are not good for cutting since they wilt quickly off the vine. There is also a variety with a white flower.

WEEPING BOTTLEBRUSH (*Callistemon viminalis*)
This large shrub, a native of Australia, grows to about 10 feet. There are several varieties of this plant and some grow into small trees. The scientific name for all of them comes from two Greek words meaning beautiful threads—a reference to the long, cylindrical spikes of bright red stamens that look like the brushes used to clean bottles. The dry fruits look like little gray buttons. This plant has the same drooping appearance as the weeping willow and does best in moist soil.

YELLOW BUTTERFLY PALM
(*Chrysalidocarpus lutescens*)
This palm, native to Madagascar, goes by a variety of names—areca palm, cane palm, and bamboo palm. It grows in clumps up to 40 feet high, with slender yellow trunks that are ringed like bamboo. It has graceful yellow green leaves. It is an old Florida favorite, used for tropical effect in outdoor landscaping and as a potted specimen for indoor show.

28. PARKS AND REFUGES

There are as many as 100 parks, refuges, and sanctuaries in south Florida, each with its own characteristic flavor and many with extensive recreational and camping facilities. Those areas described here are especially rich in species of native flora and fauna and help provide an appreciation and understanding of the fascinating natural wonders of the entire subtropical region. The list starts near Stuart on the east and then follows the coastline down to the Keys and then up along the west coast to Sarasota.

JONATHAN DICKINSON STATE PARK

This 10,000-acre park, located on U.S. 1, 13 miles south of Stuart between Jupiter and Hobe Sound, was named for the famous Quaker, Jonathan Dickinson, who, with his wife and infant child, was shipwrecked in this vicinity in 1696, discovered and harassed by Indians, and finally reached home in Philadelphia after an extremely arduous journey. Rolling, white sand dunes covered with scrub pines and palmettos level out into typical slash pine flatwoods dotted with ponds. An interesting trail is along the Loxahatchee River where mangroves and Sabal palms grow. There are guided horseback tours on miles of scenic trails and a jungle cruise on the *Loxahatchee Queen*. One of the sandy hills, Hobe Mountain, rises 86 feet above sea level, making it one of the highest natural points in south Florida. It is topped with a 22-foot observation tower.

LOXAHATCHEE NATIONAL WILDLIFE REFUGE

This ecologically unique area, a small portion of the famous Everglades, is one of the largest freshwater marshes in North America. The legendary "River of Grass," with its saw grass, marshes, wet prairies, open water sloughs, and tree islands, is spread over much of the 145,000 acres. The eastern side of the refuge includes a remnant of the cypress swamp that used to fringe the Everglades marsh. A boardwalk cuts through this swamp and its bald cypress, guava, pond apple, and an outstanding variety of ferns. The refuge provides habitat for many forms of wildlife including such endangered species as the Everglade kite, Florida panther, bald eagle, and sandhill crane. Recreational fishing is excellent. There is an excellent vantage point for watching waterfowl and other birds during the winter months at refuge headquarters, 12 miles west of Delray. Two other access points are used by the public. The 20-Mile Bend recreation area is at the north end of the refuge, accessible from U.S. 98 leading directly from West Palm Beach. The Loxahatchee area is at the south end, west of Deerfield Beach.

HUGH TAYLOR BIRCH STATE PARK

This park, in downtown Fort Lauderdale, is one of the most visited state parks in Florida. It extends along the ocean on the east. On the west it borders for a mile along the intracoastal waterway. A miniature tour train takes passengers on a three-mile ride along the ocean, along the intracoastal waterway, and over two freshwater lagoons and a park that is a botanical treasure house of subtropical trees and plants.

FAIRCHILD TROPICAL GARDEN

These 83 acres on Old Cutler Road in Coral Gables comprise the only major tropical botanical garden in the United States. It is maintained for research and educational purposes and is open to the public for study and enjoyment. Conducted tours on motorized trams help you see the many garden attractions, which include: the palmetum in which there are 500 different species of palms; the cycad circle, containing primitive seed-bearing plants that are palmlike and fernlike; a sunken garden surrounded by ferns and lush tropical plants; a rare plant house with a large collection of orchids, bromeliads, and ferns; a simulated rain forest with shade-loving jungle plants, including giant staghorn ferns growing on tree trunks; a rock garden filled with such drought-loving plants as aloes, yuccas, and agave; a vine pergola whose columns are covered with a wide variety of climbing plants; and flowering trees of many species planted in family groups.

MATHESON HAMMOCK PARK

This park adjoins Fairchild Tropical Gardens on Old Cutler Road in Coral Gables. Nature trails wind through this typical tree island. Almost all the hammock trees are visible: live oak, gumbo limbo, wild mastic, strangler fig, paradise tree, and pigeon plum. The branches of the live oaks support numerous air plants, and in the less wooded areas birds occur in considerable numbers. Hammock areas are scarce, but a few blocks south of downtown Miami, on S.W. 17th Road, one block west of South Miami Avenue, is Simpson Park, a fine example of this type of environment. The entrance sign to this park reads: "Down this path lies the Miami of the early 1900's. From the Miami River to Coconut Grove this region was one vast subtropical jungle. The conditions you see here parallel those of more than 50 years ago."

BISCAYNE NATIONAL MONUMENT

The three small islands immediately north of Key Largo are Old Rhodes Key, Elliott Key, and Sands Key. These three keys and the water and reefs surrounding them make up this national monument of approximately 95,000 acres. The area is noted for its rich marine life, for its spectacular coral reefs, and for the interaction of its temperate and tropical plants and animals. The temporary headquarters of the park are located on the mainland at Homestead Bayfront Park.

JOHN PENNEKAMP CORAL REEF STATE PARK

This incredibly beautiful park, embracing 100 square miles of the large living coral formation along the coast, was named after John D. Pennekamp, a Miami newspaperman, who was long active in preserving Florida's wilderness areas. The park is almost entirely underwater and contains 40 of the 52 species of coral found in the Atlantic reef system. The submarine growths are spawning grounds for tropical fish and other sealife. The park's feature attraction is the tour to the outer reefs in a boat designed with an underwater observation room, where the viewer is actually below the surface of the water. Other activities include snorkeling, scuba trips, canoeing, and swimming. The park headquarters are just north of Key Largo, 55 miles south of Miami.

LONG KEY STATE RECREATION AREA

Situated about 85 miles south of Miami in the so-called middle keys, this water-oriented recreation area of over 1,000 acres takes advantage of both the Atlantic Ocean and the Gulf of Mexico. The sand-covered coral island supports dense mangrove thickets, as well as a growth of tropical trees and shrubs native to the Florida Keys. A nature trail is in the northern section of the park and winds through an area adjacent to Florida Bay. A historic marker in the park recognizes the early fishing activities in this area of Zane Grey, the well-known author of many outdoor novels.

BAHIA HONDA STATE PARK

Florida's southernmost state park, located 12 miles south of Marathon and 35 miles north of Key West, has beaches on both the Atlantic Ocean and the Gulf of Mexico and a long lagoon paralleling U.S. 1. Waves, winds, and birds have brought the seeds of many tropical trees and plants from the West Indies. Some rare species have adapted well in this environment as have several unusual species of birds. Beachcombing for unusual shells is a popular pastime of visitors.

REFUGES OF THE FLORIDA KEYS

The Florida Keys are the sites of three National Wildlife Refuges: the National Key Deer Refuge, the Great White Heron Refuge, and the Key West Wildlife Refuge. Headquarters for these refuges are on Big Pine Key. The three refuges are made up of scattered islands, more or less within sight of each other, stretching for about 60 miles from the vicinity of East Bahia Honda Key on the east to the Marquesas Keys on the west. All the refuge islands are accessible only by boat, with the exception of the parts of National Key Deer Refuge on Big Pine and Little Torch Keys. The National Key Deer Refuge was established to protect the Florida Key whitetail deer, a diminutive deer that had almost reached the vanishing point 30 years ago. Over 300 species of plant life, including a rich variety of orchids and air plants, have been found on Big Pine Key. The Great White Heron Refuge gives permanent protection to the bird for which it was named and to such other rare birds as the white-crowned pigeon and the roseate spoonbill. The Key West National Wildlife Refuge affords habitat to a wide variety of birds, especially terns, frigate birds, roseate spoonbills, white-crowned pigeons, ospreys, and great white herons.

FORT JEFFERSON NATIONAL MONUMENT

About seventy miles west of Key West is a group of seven small islands called the Dry Tortugas. These westernmost Florida Keys, picturesquely set in clear blue waters, and the surrounding shoals make up this national monument. These islands are steeped in early American naval history, as evidenced by the dramatic brick ruins of Fort Jefferson on Garden Key. Though these islands can be reached only by boat or seaplane, they are well known to snorkelers and scuba divers for the colorful coral beds, to sport and commercial fishermen for the variety of the available species, and to ornithologists for the abundance of the bird life, especially the spectacular nesting sites of the sooty and noddy terns.

EVERGLADES NATIONAL PARK

This park, 1.4 million acres, was established to protect for this and future generations a sprawling subtropical wilderness, a complex of unique plant-and-animal communities threatened with destruction. Some of the habitats, such as the Everglades themselves, and some of the animals—crocodile, manatee, roseate spoonbill, reddish egret, and bald eagle—are rare and generally unseen elsewhere in the United States. Among other plant and animal inhabitants are the alligator, snook, tarpon, pink shrimp, royal palm, mahogany, and mangroves. This great biological exhibit in an aquatic setting presents a living drama of nature in unspoiled surroundings. The main entrance to the park is 35 miles southeast of Miami and 12 miles from Homestead on State Route 27. The Visitor Center near the park entrance should not be bypassed, for here are exhibits, films, publications, and talks by park interpreters. A highway leads through the heart of the park, with self-guided walking trails through the principal habitats: sloughs, hammocks, pinelands, glades, and mangrove swamps. At the end of the highway is Flamingo, where a variety of land and water tours are offered. The western gateway to the park at Everglades City is the boater's entrance to the waters of the Ten Thousand Islands and the Gulf Coast—a mecca for sport fishermen. Daily boat tours are operated from the park docks on Chokoloskee Causeway on State Road 29. The third entrance to the park is on the Tamiami Trail, U.S. 41, where at Shark Valley Loop Road a two-hour guided tram tour explores seven miles into the interior of the glades.

COLLIER SEMINOLE STATE PARK

The Big Cypress Swamp joins the Everglades at this park. This was the last refuge of the Seminole Indians, and there are still some Indian villages nearby. The 6,500 acre preserve is located 20 miles northeast of Everglades City on the Tamiami Trail, U.S. 41. From a boat basin near the park's entrance, boaters can reach the Gulf via a canal going into Blackwater River, affording a beautiful trip down a wilderness stream through the Ten Thousand Islands. A well-marked nature trail makes a large loop among the native plants, shrubs, and some magnificent royal palms. The park was named for Baron Collier who displayed much interest in this locality and its history.

ROOKERY BAY WILDLIFE SANCTUARY

This sanctuary, maintained by the Audubon Society, lies within the Ten Thousand Islands which stretch from Naples to Cape Sable. It is an unspoiled estuary, in effect a huge nutrient trap where fertile freshwater from the upland meets life-giving minerals from the Gulf of Mexico. This makes it an ideal nursery for fish, shellfish, waterfowl, wading birds, and shorebirds. Brown pelicans, osprey, and bald eagles rear their young in this subtropical sanctuary. Winged visitors of tropical America mingle with those nesting on the Arctic Circle. The sanctuary is best toured by boat as all but a few hundred acres are subject to tidal flooding. Boats may be rented at Naples or Marco Island, and the sanctuary is easily reached by well-marked waterways from these points.

CORKSCREW SWAMP SANCTUARY

At the northern tip of the Big Cypress Swamp lies a wilderness area of some 10,000 acres containing this country's largest remaining stand of virgin bald cypress, the oldest trees in eastern North America, some of them 700 years old. This sanctuary, owned and operated by the National Audubon Society, gives shelter to some of the largest flocks of endangered wildfowl in North America. A mile-long boardwalk takes visitors across a wet prairie and into a primeval wilderness of the big tree area, with silvery Spanish moss, orchids, ferns, and ponds overgrown with water lettuce. At nesting time large flocks of wood ibis and egrets cover the treetops like a gleaming white canopy. The sanctuary is on State Road 846 between Immokalee and Naples.

J. N. "DING" DARLING NATIONAL WILDLIFE REFUGE

Sanibel Island, known for its world-famous shell beaches, is 15 miles southwest of Fort Myers on State Road 867 and is reached over a causeway stretching three miles into the Gulf of Mexico. The refuge lies mainly on the north shore of this island and covers over 5,000 acres. The refuge was established for the purpose of providing habitat for migratory ducks and other birds at the southern end of the Atlantic flyway. Thousands of ducks winter here. It is also a summer nesting site for mottled ducks, black-necked stilts, and gallinules, as well as the more common herons, egrets, anhingas, pelicans, and the rare roseate spoonbills. The center of the refuge is a favorite night roost for two or three thousand herons, egrets, and ibises.

MYAKKA RIVER STATE PARK

Florida's largest state park covers some 28,000 acres and includes pine flatwoods, palmetto prairies, hammocks, marshes, lakes, and the Myakka River. The diversity of aquatic areas and the vastness of the park account for the great abundance of species, especially wading birds and waterfowl. Ospreys, bald eagles, sandhill cranes, deer, and wild pigs are commonly seen. A concession boat tour on the lake is provided when water levels permit. A tram provides a tour of the hardwood hammock and river floodplain. A 7,500-acre wilderness preserve resembles Florida as it looked before the arrival of European man. A limited number of visitors are allowed to visit this preserve each day on foot. The park is 17 miles east of Sarasota on State Road 72.

Southern Cross

Great-horned Owl

Green
Tree Frog

Night-blooming
Cereus
(a cactus flower)

Squirrel
Tree Frog

Spider
Lily

String or
Swamp Lily

Night-blooming
Epidendrum

Luna Moth

Spotted
Skunk

Bobcat

Striped Skunk

Evening Primrose

Moonflower

Moth (with
siphon extended)

Night

29. NIGHT

When the evening primrose opens its yellow flowers, night is about to fall. In the last glow of the sun black skimmers will glide down over the surface of the bays to scoop up fish, and the common nighthawk will open his wide mouth to capture flying insects on the wing. Most wading birds will take to the woody thickets on the salt marshes for a night of rest. Gulls will sleep on the beaches or on the islets in the bays or float gently on other still waters. But the night heron who has slept most of the day will begin his nocturnal search for food. Owls, with their large immovable eyes in their swollen feathered faces, will flex their curved claws in preparation for the hunt. Many of them, including the great horned owl, who is one of the largest and most powerful of his clan, will often hunt in the daytime as well as during the night, disproving the common notion that owls cannot see in the sunlight. Owls perform somewhat the same beneficial service as birds—the destruction of pests that plague people.

Down on the beach a different type of activity takes place. Sand hoppers come out of their daytime burrows and go down to the sea wrack for food. When finished they will return to the higher part of the dune to excavate new burrows. Other beach insects congregate in the decaying wrack. Wolf spiders and ghost crabs leave their shelters to run down these insects. Although ghost crabs live in the sandy beach, they still breathe through gills and must go regularly to the water's edge to moisten up. They are in the process of switching from seafarers to landlubbers. The nighttime beach also attracts larger animals. Rats and raccoons come down to the wrack and the tide pools to forage in the debris for crabs, worms, fish, and other food. The raccoon will wash his food vigorously before eating it, not for cleanliness but apparently because he likes to feel the food in water.

A remarkable sight occurs in May and June on nights of the "spring" tides, which occur at new-moon and full-moon times, or every two weeks. During these tides, the level of the water rises higher and falls lower than usual. On these nights horseshoe crabs, the larger females carrying males on their backs, come ashore at high tide. The females lay eggs in the sand, while the waves wash the sperm of the males over the eggs to fertilize them. When the tide ebbs, the crabs return to the water. At the next spring tide, two weeks later, the young larvae are flushed into the water to begin their scramble to maturity.

Nighttime is the signal for a chorus of sounds in which a variety of insects and animals participate. Several species of crickets and grasshoppers "sing" most actively by night. The males produce their distinctive trills and buzzes by rubbing their front wings together. The most vocal orchestrations are provided by the frogs.

Every kind makes its own music, from the vibrant chirps of the small chorus frog to the resonant croak of the large bullfrog. The voices of the tree frogs are loud, clear, and musical. These are the frogs often seen at night plastered to Florida window screens, feeding on mosquitos. They owe their agility to specialized sticky toe pads, permitting them to swing from twig to twig in their nocturnal search for food. The most attractive is the uniformly light green, long-legged green tree frog. The squirrel tree frog is smaller and has changeable colors. Just as the birds give the daytime its sounds, the night is dominated by the voices of the frogs, with an occasional drumbeat from a bellowing alligator. Many of these native frogs are now threatened by the giant toad, *Bufo marinus*. This warty creature of the night, an exotic species accidentally introduced from Latin America, has found Florida a cordial and salubrious environment. Poisonous glands in the back of its head make it an unappetizing prey, while with its own enormous appetite it keeps devouring anything in sight including other amphibians.

There are many native animals that also do their hunting at night. One of these is the small spotted skunk, distinguished by the broken white stripes on its black body. Another is the striped skunk, whose identifying mark is the large white patch along the top of its back. The scent glands of these animals protect them from molesters. Among the larger nighttime hunters is the bobcat. The phrase "lick his weight in wildcats" is a tribute to this ferocious fighter that will not hesitate to do battle with enemies twice its size. Except for its short tail and tufted cheeks, it looks like an overgrown housecat. Other animals most active at night are the armadillo and the opossum.

Night also has its impact on various botanical species. Several spectacular flowers do not bloom until the sun has set. One of these is moonflower or moonvine, a vigorous plant that climbs over everything. During the day its flowers hang limply among the heart-shaped leaves. These are the daily casualties of those that blossomed the night before. In the evening new buds open quickly into large white flowers, shaped like morning glories, with a strong fragrance that attracts several kinds of colorful moths. These moths insert their tongues into the flower tubes to extract nectar, and in the process cross pollinate the plants.

Another plant that produces blossoms that last only until the next morning is the night-blooming cereus. This cactus, with fleshy, triangular, spiny stems uses its aerial roots to climb trees, banks, and walls. Huge buds open in the summer evenings into heavily perfumed, magnificent flowers that wilt and die in the heat of the following morning. Because of the short-lived appearance of its blossoms, this cactus is sometimes called the cinderella plant. The evening primrose, another nocturnal species, is a low-spreading plant found in sandy areas. Its yellow blossoms open late in the afternoon, are pollinated by moths, and then lose color and wilt by noon of the following day.

Some plants produce flowers that remain open for several days but have special nocturnal habits. Two members of the amaryllis family fall into this category; the string or swamp lily and the spider lily both attract their pollinating moths by heavily intensifying their fragrances beginning at sunset. The night-blooming epidendrum, a beautiful orchid, does not depend on any moth for survival. Its name comes from the special nighttime fragrance of its white, spiderlike blossoms.

All this nighttime activity moves along under a canopy dotted with brilliant stars. Those that are visible at any specific hour depend upon the location of the viewer, the time of night, and the season of the year. In southern Florida one if the most unique constellations is the sparkling Southern Cross. The most awesome and sublime sight of all is the Milky Way—a majestic spectacle of the infinite bowl of space that envelops humans and their tiny world.

INDEX